(continued from front flap)

the Old and the New Testaments is entirely free from the prejudices and arbitrary decisions of the partisan scholar. Her interest lies in explaining to the reader the very human evolution of religion from nature worship to the belief in the warm and living God of the prophets, culminating in Christ. Her lucid review of the origins, selection, and ordering of the Bible's contents gives the reader a sure understanding of this evolutionary process and a profound sense of the continuity of basic religious thought. For those who are seeking a fresh perspective of the Bible, this dignified and reverent study will be an invaluable guide.

Mallory Beattie is the pen name of Mrs. Hazel Mallory Beattie Rogers. Mrs. Rogers and her husband, an attorney, live in Tulsa, Oklahoma, where she is active in the First Christian Church and in many other organizations. She is a member of the American Association of University Women, the League of Women Voters, the Shakespearean Society, and the Women's Association of Tulsa Boys' Home.

The author of *The Making of the Old and the New Testaments* was born in Dover, Missouri. She is a graduate of the University of Oklahoma (Phi Beta Kappa), and holds an M.A. from the University of Arizona.

THE MAKING OF
THE OLD AND THE NEW TESTAMENTS

THE MAKING OF THE OLD AND THE NEW TESTAMENTS

A HISTORICAL STUDY BY

Mallory Beattie

EXPOSITION PRESS · NEW YORK

FIRST EDITION

*

*All rights reserved including the right of
reproduction in whole or in part in any form*
Copyright, 1953, by Mallory Beattie
Published by the Exposition Press Inc.
386 Fourth Avenue, New York 16, N. Y.
Designed by Ruth London
Manufactured in the United States of America
Consolidated Book Producers, Inc.
Library of Congress catalog card number: 53-11268

TO

JOHN *and* JOHNNIE

Acknowledgments

Grateful acknowledgment for permission to quote from the listed copyright works is made—

To the Abingdon-Cokesbury Press, for Walter Russell Bowie's *The Story of the Bible*

To Irma Fall Brightman and Jannette E. Newhall, executrices of the estate of Edgar Sheffield Brightman, for his *The Sources of the Hexateuch*

To the publisher Christophers (London), for Kirsopp Lake's *Paul, His Heritage and Legacy*

To Columbia University Press, for Julius A. Bewer's *The Literature of the Old Testament in Its Historical Development* and for Ernest Findlay Scott's *The Literature of the New Testament*

To E. P. Dutton and Company, for Joseph H. Wicksteed's *A Study of Blake's Vision of the Book of Job*

To Edgar J. Goodspeed, for his *New Chapters in New Testament Study*

To Harvard University Press, for George Foot Moore's *Judaism in the First Centuries of the Christian Era.*

To J. B. Lippincott Company, for Morris Jastrow, Jr.'s *A Gentle Cynic*

To the Macmillan Company (New York), for Henry Thatcher Fowler's *The History and Literature of the New Testament* and for John Merlin Powis Smith's *The Books of Amos, Hosea and Micah*

To Macmillan and Company, Ltd. (London), for Herbert Edward Ryle's *The Canon of the Old Testament*

To Henry Holt and Company, for Albert Schweitzer's *The Mysticism of Paul the Apostle*

To Charles Scribner's Sons, for Henry Kendall Booth's *The Background of the Bible,* for Martin Dibelius' *A Fresh Approach to the New Testament and Early Christian Literature,* for Mary Ely Lyman's *The Christian Epic,* for Ernest Findlay Scott's *The Gospel and Its Tributaries* and *The New Testament Idea of Revelation,* and for Alexander Souter's *The Text and Canon of the New Testament*

To the Union of American Hebrew Congregations, for Cecil Roth's *A Bird's-Eye View of Jewish History*

To the University of Chicago Press, for Edgar J. Goodspeed's *The Formation of the New Testament, New Solutions of New Testament Problems, The Story of the Bible,* and *The Story of the New Testament*

Contents

Introduction

The ancient Jews classified the writings of the Old Testament under three heads: the Law, the Prophets, and the Writings (or Torah, Nebiim, Kethubim). To account for this triple division we must understand how the Old Testament canon took shape.

Circumstances attending the growth of the Old Testament canon were as widely different as possible from those which accompanied the formation of the New Testament canon. The canon of the New Testament was formed by gradual accretion, and its limits were determined by popular usage rather than by personal or official authority.[1]

To account for the circumstances attending the growth of the canon of the Old and the New Testaments is the purpose of this study. In accounting for this growth it will be necessary to explain the contradictions and apparent inconsistencies within the Old and the New Testaments, and to explain the presence of curious duplications and repetitions in many narratives. The three stages of the Hebrew canon will be discussed: the formation of the literary antecedents of the books; the compilation and reduction to their present literary form; the final selection for the position of honor and sanctity in the national canon of Holy Scripture. A similar procedure will be followed in the discussion of the New Testament canon, with these questions in mind: Who wrote each book? Why and in what circumstances was it written? With what materials? And, for whom?

At the inception of this study we ask ourselves these questions: How did the Bible come into being? What are the raw materials out of which sprang the Bible in relation to the new whole which was wrought from them? How did the Council of Jamnia, in A.D. 90, settle the question of the canon of the Old Testament? How did the New Testament take its definite form

---

[1] See H. E. Ryle, *The Canon of the Old Testament,* pp. 8–9.

when in A.D. 367 Athanasius enumerated the twenty-seven books as we now have them in the New Testament?

To show the progressive revelation of God which these questions imply, we must necessarily discuss the raw material out of which the Bible was formed. This quest for the raw material or the sources of the Bible started in the eighteenth century when a French physician, Jean Astruc, noted in our Pentateuch (Law, or Torah) variations in the names of Jehovah and Elohim. This led him to distinguish two main documents in the Pentateuch: the first, or Elohistic, or E and P; the second, or Jahvistic, or J. Astruc did not question at that time the Mosaic authorship of the Pentateuch (the Law).

The first separation of P and E into the Priestly and the Elohistic sources was made by Segen, in 1789. But not until 1806 did De Wette establish the date of the publication of Deuteronomy as 621 B.C. on the basis of II Kings 22–23. He regarded the entire Law or Pentateuch as a single development.[2]

Not until the middle of the nineteenth century did Hupfield hold that J, E, and P were independent sources, and that J, in particular, did not know P. In 1866, Graf proved that P was postexilic.

In 1876, Wellhausen initiated a systematic interpretation of Israelitic history and religion on the basis of the analysis of the Hexateuch (or the first six books of the Old Testament) into J, E, D (Deuteronomy, in its original form), and P. Scholars agree that he was right in his analysis and in his dating of the documents. Scholars distinguish between the various documents or texts J, E, D, and P by their difference in language, style, ideas and content.

Before we take up the discussion of the four documents, J, E, D, P, in the following chapter, we shall need to know a few of the historical facts which brought about the writing of the documents. From the desert country around Palestine, a group of nomad tribes emerged (about 1150 B.C.) to make Palestine their home. These tribes worshipped a God whom they called Yahweh and whom they believed to be, in some

_____
[2] See E. S. Brightman, *The Sources of the Hexateuch*, p. 13.

sense, localized at Mount Sinai in northern Arabia. The name *God* in Hebrew consists of four consonants, JHVH, or YHWH. This name was considered by the Jews too holy to pronounce. Instead, they said "The Lord" (hence the usage of the King James Version). This led the Jews to pronounce JHVH with the vowels belonging to the word *Lord* (in Hebrew, *Adonai*). Hence there arose the traditional vocalization Yahweh, or Jehovah.[3] Yahweh was a destructive god, manifesting himself in storm, earthquake, volcano, and war. Morality in the minds of these tribes had no connection with the religion of Yahweh. But Moses taught his people that God was interested in their everyday life and in justice between man and man and between clan and clan.

In the eighth century the prophets arose to proclaim the majesty and transcendency of Yahweh. These prophets taught that Israel existed for God, not God for Israel. Doom awaited a people who had turned aside from God. The predictions of the prophets Amos and Hosea were fulfilled. The Northern Kingdom fell before the Assyrians in 722 B.C., but the Southern Kingdom remained, though a vassal state of the Assyrian empire, for more than a hundred years. When the Northern Kingdom disappeared, as the prophets had said that it would, respect for the prophets, especially in the Southern Kingdom, was increased.

The Persians in 538 B.C. gained control of the Babylonian empire and re-established Jerusalem as the national and religious center. The exclusiveness which had been built up among the exiles was enforced in the Palestinian community. Ruth and Jonah are protests against an extreme form of this exclusiveness. When the Priestly code was adopted (Ezra, Nehemiah, Chronicles), the people had ceased to be a nation and had become a church.

These historical facts were incorporated in the four documents, for J was written in the Southern Kingdom in the ninth century; E was written in the Northern Kingdom in the eighth century; D was published in 621 B.C.; and P was written during the Exile. J, E, D, and P were interwoven during the Exile, and

[3] See Brightman, *op. cit.*, p. 18.

from this editing or compilation the Jewish Law (Genesis, Exodus, Leviticus, Numbers, and Deuteronomy) was derived.

The first part of the Old Testament canon is the Law (the
Torah, equivalent to our Pentateuch), which is the most holy.
The Law is made up of five books—Genesis, Exodus, Leviticus,
Numbers, and Deuteronomy—and was completed about 444 B.C.
The Prophets, or the second section, completed about 200 B.C.,
consists of twenty-one books: Joshua, Judges, I Samuel, II
Samuel, I Kings, II Kings, Isaiah, Jeremiah, Ezekiel, Hosea,
Joel, Amos, Obadiah, Jonah, Micah, Nahum, Habakkuk, Zephaniah, Haggai, Zechariah, and Malachi. The Former Prophets
included the books of Joshua, Judges, I and II Samuel, and
I and II Kings. The Latter Prophets consisted of material grouped
into four sections, Isaiah, Jeremiah, Ezekiel, and the twelve
minor prophets. The Writings were completed about 100 B.C.
This third section of the Old Testament canon consists of thirteen books: Psalms, Proverbs, Job, Song of Songs, Ruth, Lamentations, Ecclesiastes, Esther, Daniel, Ezra, Nehemiah, I Chronicles and II Chronicles. The Writings, in a Hebrew Bible, are
divided into three groups: the poetical books are Psalms, Proverbs and Job; the five festival rolls are the Song of Songs, Ruth,
Lamentations, Ecclesiastes, and Esther; the remaining books are
Daniel, Ezra, Nehemiah, I Chronicles and II Chronicles.[4]

For many centuries the whole Jewish and Chistian world
believed that the Hebrew Scriptures were an exact dictation
from Heaven and that the Hebrew language used in the Bible
was God's own choice vocabulary. Today, it is impossible to
speak of the Hebrew of the Old Testament as if it were all of a
piece. Some of the writers used Palestinian-Hebrew, others
Babylonian-Hebrew, and still others Aramaic-Hebrew, types
that differ as widely as the English of Milton from that of Ber-
nard Shaw. We know, then, that different authors characterized
by differences in diction and style wrote the Law, and not
Moses. Internal evidence within the Law, or the Pentateuch,
also indicates that Moses could not have been the exclusive
author of the five books commonly ascribed to him.

---

[4] See James Hastings, *Dictionary of the Bible*, p. 112.

Since the Jews classified the Old Testament under three heads—the Law, the Prophets, and the Writings—we shall separate this study of the Old Testament into three chapters, naming them as follows: Chapter I, "The Law"; Chapter II, "The Prophets"; and Chapter III, "The Writings." In the study of the Law we shall show how the five books which comprise the Law (Genesis, Exodus, Leviticus, Numbers, Deuteronomy) are a compilation of the various sources or documents J, E, D, and P.

Just as the five books of the Law are editorial compilations, so are the Prophetic books. Isaiah, Amos, Hosea, and Micah prophesied for their contemporaries, and their prophecies were written down, partly by their disciples, and preserved. Hundreds of years later, editors, in order to bring these books and truths up to modern conditions, edited them by interpolating their own comments. It is our purpose in Chapter II to show just how this was accomplished.

The prophets were represented as alternating their prophecies of doom with messages proclaiming the future glory of the nation. This Messianic belief forms one of the chief links between the Old and the New Testaments. The Old Testament points forward to Christ in that certain passages speak of a coming deliverer and in the progressive self-revelation of God, which finds completion in the Incarnation.

A similar editing of the Writings took place. In the Prophets, the first history of the Jewish monarchy was written in Judges, I Samuel, II Samuel, I Kings, and II Kings. But in the Writings a second history was written in I Chronicles, II Chronicles, Ezra, and Nehemiah in the light of the P Code. This editing will be dealt with in Chapter III.

Part Two, on the making of the New Testament, considers the material divided into four sections: (1) the Synoptic Gospels—the Gospels according to Matthew, Mark, and Luke (Acts is considered with Luke, for originally it was a sequel to Luke); (2) the Johannine Writings—the Gospel according to John, Revelation, I John, II John, and III John; (3) the letters other than Paul's; and (4) Paul's letters.

The order of the King James Version will be followed when

possible; but when necessary, this scheme has been subject to change. Not all of the books of the Bible will be discussed in this study, for it has been necessary to select and discriminate. In quoting from the Bible, the Authorized Version has been used, except in a few passages [5] where, for the sake of clarity, the Revised Version was used.

Throughout this discussion we shall show that the Bible is a finished work, the result of centuries of selection, of revision, and of editing, and that behind both the Old and the New Testaments there is a large body of literature which was never accepted as canonical. Through the study of the origin and nature of the books of the Bible we shall also see the form of primitive Hebrew worship, with animal sacrifices, change to the magnificent understanding of the prophets' idea of God. We shall watch this expanding vision until we find it climaxed in Christ and his teachings.

The following tables will clarify the history and literature behind the making of the Old and the New Testaments: [6]

------

[5] Whenever the Revised Version is used, we call attention to this fact in a footnote.

[6] These tables are from Professor S. F. Pattison's course, *The Bible as Literature*, University of Arizona.

Old Testament History and Literature

Period of Biblical History	Documents
Patriarchal Era 2040–1600 B.C.	
Settlement in Egypt 1600–1200 B.C.	
Period of Wanderings 1200–1150 B.C.	
Settlement in Palestine 1150–1037 B.C.	
United Kingdom 1037–938 B.C.	
Divided Kingdom 938–586 B.C.	Primitive codes { J (850 B.C.) / E (750 B.C.) / JE (650 B.C.) } Deuteronomic code D (621 B.C.)
Babylonian Exile 586–537 B.C.	Ezekiel's code Holiness code
Persian Rule 537–332 B.C.	JED (520 B.C.) Priestly code P (450 B.C.)
Greek Rule 332–320 B.C.	All of the above codes incorporated (a) in our Pentateuch (the Law) in 444 B.C., (b) in Joshua, Judges, I and II Samuel, and I and II Kings in 340 B.C., and (c) in I and II Chronicles, Ezra, and Nehemiah in 250 B.C.
Egyptian Rule 320–200 B.C.	
Syrian Rule 200–142 B.C.	

Important Events in Old Testament History
(All Dates B.C.)

KINGS OF JUDAH	DATE (B.C.)	KINGS OF ISRAEL	CONTEMPORARIES
Amaziah	797		
	785	Jeroboam II	
			Shalmaneser IV of Assyria (783–773)
Uzziah	770		
Jotham	750	Zachariah	
	749	Shallum	
	749	Menahem	Tiglath-pileser (Pul) II of Assyria (745–727)
	738	Pekahiah	Rezin of Syria
	736	Pekah	
Ahaz	734		
	730	Hosea	
Hezekiah	727		Shalmaneser V of Assyria (727–722)
	722	Fall of Samaria	Sargon II of Assyria (705–681)
			Sennacherib of Assyria (705–681)
Manasseh	698		
			Esarhaddon, son of Sennacherib, of Assyria (681–668) conquers Egypt in 670
Amon	642		Ashurbanipal of Assyria (668–626)
Josiah	640		
			Cyaxares founded the Median empire (633)

Kings of Judah	Date (B.C.)	Kings of Israel	Contemporaries
			The Scythian invasion (626)
			Nabopolassar, king of Babylon (625–605)
Jehoahaz	608		Pharaoh–necoh of Egypt (609–594)
Jehoiakim	608		Nebuchadrezzar II of Babylon (604–561)
Jehoiachin	597		
Zedekiah	597		
Fall of Jerusalem	586		

PART ONE

The Old Testament

· I ·

The Law (the Pentateuch)

The Hebrew Bible represents a process of consecutive addition, comprising three distinct sections, each completed in a particular age and carrying its own rank and holiness just one step or degree above the other. These three sections are the Law, the Prophets, the Writings. This triple division indicates three different stages in the process which finally resulted in the completed Hebrew Scriptures.

The three stages cannot be understood until some of the sources from which the Old Testament were derived are understood. The sources which we shall discuss are the documents J, E, D, and P, and each document will be discussed in the order named. How these documents are interwoven to form the Pentateuch (the Law, or the Torah) is our second consideration in this chapter, for the Law is a collection of the J, E, D, P documents representing successive periods in the national life of Israel. These independent sources were worked over by a succession of editors, or redactors, designated by R, who treated their material in different ways. When two or more of the sections told the same story with variations, they would sometimes interweave the respective accounts.

The J (Jahvistic or Judean narrative) was written about 850 B.C. The E (Elohistic or Ephraimitic narrative) was written about 750 B.C. The D (Deuteronomy, in its original form) was written about 650 B.C. and published in 621 B.C. The P (Priestly code) was written about 500 B.C. The J and E documents were combined by editors or redactors (R_{je}) about 650 B.C., and their finished work is called JE. JE and D were combined by editors or redactors (R_d), and these redactors also made additions to D about 600–550 B.C.; this finished work was called JED. The Law, or Pentateuch, was put into its present form by redactors who united JED with P, about 400 B.C.[1]

THE J MATERIAL

The J material is a unit in thought, expression and mood, in social and ethical outlook, and in historical background. The J narrative was written in the ninth century in the Southern Kingdom, and this literature belongs together as contrasted with the E, D, and P types.

Critics agree that the J material may be found in Genesis, Exodus, Numbers, and Joshua. There is no J material in Leviticus and only a very little prefixed to Deuteronomy. Most critics treat Judges 2:5 as the last trace of J. The collecting of these legends and preserving them in writing extended over a long period of time and was, therefore, given to us in the present state by many minds and hands. We distinguish two stages in this process: the older, to which we owe the collections of the Jahvists, designated by J, and the Elohist, designated by E, and then a later, thorough revision in what is known as the Priestly codex, P. The theme of these books of legends is "The choice of Israel to be the people of Jahveh." [2]

J furnishes the greatest amount of material in Genesis, including the stories of Adam and Eve, Abraham, Isaac, and Jacob. J is a poet of the grand style. He is vivid, picturesque, and concrete and is unsurpassed as a storyteller and in delineat-

---

[1] See E. S. Brightman, *The Sources of the Hexateuch*, p. 10.
[2] Hermann Gunkel, *The Legends of Genesis*, p. 124.

ing character with deft touches of charm and beauty. J, in Genesis, contains two parallel pedigrees of race: the Cainite genealogy and the Sethite line (Genesis 5:29). In combining the first and second genealogy, a third is introduced, which comes from the legend of Cain and Abel.

J and E belong essentially to the same period. They are closely related, but the difference between them is in the use of language. J uses the name Jahveh before the time of Moses, while E uses Elohim.[3] J in Genesis 2:4 uses the name Jehovah. E mentions it first in Exodus 3, and P mentions it first in Exodus 6. Other proper names used by J in contrast to E are Israel (as a later name of Jacob) and Canaanite (for E's Amorite). J emphasizes the characteristic Hebrew words for *entreat, begat, before, from the time that, know, hasten, Lord* (*Adonai*), *until, oath, maid, man,* and *wife.*[4]

J holds to an unbroken continuity of the revelation from Genesis 4:26 on.[5] "The sceptre shall not depart from Judah, nor a lawgiver from between his feet, until Shiloh come; and unto him shall the gathering of the people be."[6]

J was an optimist, for he attempted to solve the problems of sickness, death, evil and work. He portrayed things idealistically —not realistically—and his conception of Jehovah was anthropomorphic, a Jehovah who walked in the garden in the cool of the day.

J tolerates no other gods than Jehovah in Israel and prepares the way for the moral monotheism of Amos.

> And Moses said unto the judges of Israel, Slay ye every one of his men that were joined unto Baal-peor. And, behold, one of the children of Israel came and brought unto his brethren a Midianitish woman in the sight of Moses, and in the sight of all the congregation of the children of Israel. . . . And when Phinehas, the son of

---

[3] *Ibid.*, p. 133.

[4] See Brightman, *op. cit.*, p. 23.

[5] *Ibid.*, p. 24. In this statement Brightman refers to Carpenter and Hartford as his source.

[6] Genesis 49:10, which is regarded as Messianic.

Eleazar, the son of Aaron the priest, saw it, he rose up from among the congregation, and took a javelin in his hand; And he went after the man of Israel into the tent, and thrust both of them through, the man of Israel, and the woman through her belly. So the plague was stayed from the children of Israel.[7]

In many cases we are unable to distinguish the two sources J and E by vocabulary. Our only guide is that variants from the two sources when they present essentially the same stories show the individual differences in their content. In J, Isaac is deceived by Jacob by means of the smell of Esau's garments. In E, Isaac is deceived by skins. Again, in J, Joseph is sold by the Ishmaelites to an Egyptian householder, while in E he is sold by Midianites to Potiphar. J's version is older than E's. J's lively, objective narrative is in contrast to E's sentimental presentation of the sacrifice of Isaac, Jacob's tenderness for his grandchildren, and the expulsion of Ishmael. E hints at the reign of Joseph:

And his brethren said to him, Shalt thou indeed reign over us? or shalt thou indeed have dominion over us? And they hated him yet the more for his dreams, and for his words.[8]

J reverences the ancient shrines at Hebron, Bethel, Shechem and Beersheba. "Thrice in the year shall all your menchildren appear before the Lord God, the God of Israel." [9] From this sentence we see J's attitude toward the three annual feasts. He recognizes the function of sacrifice, but his altars are primarily for prayer. He is more interested in righteousness than ritual. "J represents the prophetic movement at a time before its literary exponents had arisen." [10] He thinks of Israel in relation to

---

[7] Numbers 25:5–8.

[8] Genesis 37:8 is taken by Hermann Gunkel, *The Legends of Genesis*, p. 135, to mean that E's home is in the Northern Kingdom and that he is hinting at the reign of Joseph. J was written in the Southern Kingdom, according to Wellhausen, Dillman, Cornhill, Budde, Kittel, E. Meyer, Stode, and Holzinger.

[9] Exodus 34:23.

[10] Brightman, *op. cit.*, p. 26.

the other great nations of the world. His concern is with the working out of the divine purpose. J pictures the conquest of Canaan as a slow, painful process, only gradually accomplished by bands of Hebrews under no central leadership—in contrast to E and P.

The date of J is 850 B.C., while the date of E is 750 B.C. J was older than the earliest literary prophets, Amos and Hosea. J was written in the Southern Kingdom in a time of national peace and prosperity. The J narrative deals with events from the creation to the entrance of kings. A revised version of J followed in about a hundred years (750 B.C.) and is called the E document. The two are interwoven, as we shall show.

THE E MATERIAL

E begins with the promise to Abraham [11] and ends with the national assembly,[12] but E's greatest contribution is the story of Joseph. Smed holds that E carries history to the fall of Samaria in 722 B.C.[13] There is a single personality and plan back of E, yet E is less concrete and vivid and more reflective and artificial than J. E's dominant idea is that God is the supreme ruler of Israel. His God is less anthropomorphic, more spiritual, than J's. E gives us the great ideas of the prophetic movement. His heroes are Joseph and Joshua, and his interests are in the shrines of the Northern Kingdom, for the E document was written in the Northern Kingdom.

J and E give parallel accounts of the same history, yet E adds a few facts not found in J. Critics agree that E had J before him, improving that version.[14] Critics, with the exception of Erdman, are agreed that J did not compose his narrative out of his imagination. He drew on ancient oral tradition. The story

---

[11] Genesis 15.
[12] Joshua 24.
[13] Brightman, *op. cit.*, p. 112.
[14] E. S. Brightman, *The Sources of the Hexateuch*, pp. 121–22, tells us that Wellhausen, Kuenen, E. Meyer, B. Luther, Smed, George Foote Moore, and Dillman agree upon the literary dependence of E upon J. Gunkel and Eichrodt deny this dependence.

of the birth of the sons of Jacob must have been in existence
even before the works of J and E. The writing of these traditions
took place at a period which was generally disposed to authorship, when there was a fear that oral traditions might die out if
they were not preserved.[15] The collection of these legends in
writing was not perfected by one person or at one period but in
the course of a very long process by many persons. A. Lods
calls J a school, not an author. Gunkel calls J and E collectors,
not authors, and says that J has not copied from E, or E from J,
but that they had a common original source.[16]

The E (Elohim) document begins with Abraham and runs
largely parallel to J, though on occasions there are marked devi-
ations. Genesis 39 and 49 reveal divergent stories employed by
J. In the E document we can see ideas of progress in revelation.
For example, E tells us that the forefathers of the Israelites were
idolators.[17] E recognizes further progress under Moses [18] in contrast to J.[19] E, therefore, stresses the importance of Moses more
than J does. E shows a higher ethic and theology than J.[20] E's
patriarchs are on a grander scale.[21]

Most critics lay stress on at least two strata in E, which they
call E_1 and E_2; but Smed holds to the unity of E and separates
J into J_1 and J_2, a separation already recognized by most
scholars in Genesis 1–11.[22]

J and E were united later than the first half of the eighth
century by an editor R_{je}. This collector dates near the end of
the kingdom of Judah. The union took place before the addition
of the later books of legends referred to as P (the Priestly
code). It took place when great world crises were threatening
the existence of Israel and when the faith of the people was
clinging to these promises, probably from the Chaldean period.

---

[15] See Gunkel, *op. cit.*, p. 123.
[16] See Gunkel, *op. cit.*, p. 127.
[17] Joshua 24:2; Genesis 31:19; Genesis 35:2–4.
[18] Exodus 3:13–15.
[19] Genesis 4:26.
[20] Genesis 20:12; 21:12; 31:9; 45:5; 50:20.
[21] Genesis 20:7; 48:22.
[22] Brightman, *op. cit.*, p. 14.

Occasionally we find a trace of D, or the Deuteronomic, style:

> And the Lord said, Shall I hide from Abraham that thing which I do; seeing that Abraham shall surely become a great and mighty nation, and all the nations of the world shall be blessed in him? [23]

THE D MATERIAL

The D material (Deuteronomy in its original form) was written about 650 B.C., but was not published until 621 B.C. The D, or Deuteronomic, document brought together the legislative material in 650 B.C. However, the beginnings of the Old Testament canon can be dated 621 B.C. when the Book of the Law was found by workmen in the Temple. This was not the whole Jewish Torah, or our Pentateuch, but was a portion of our Deuteronomy, or a collection of laws, Deuteronomic in tone. It was found in the eighteenth year of the reign of King Josiah.

The Deuteronomic Book of the Law presupposed a knowledge of the older laws, a knowledge of the early history of the Israelitish race. The writings on which Deuteronomy depends for historical facts are Deuteronomy 1:9–17, 2:26–32, Exodus 18, and Numbers 20 and 21. The writings on which Deuteronomy depends for laws are Exodus 20–23 and the J and E narratives, which had, before the seventh century B.C., been united into a single composite work.[24] J and E were prefixed to the Deuteronomic Laws.

In the latter part of the seventh century, a program of reform was published (Deuteronomy).

> An attempt was made to formulate and put into a code of precepts the ethical teaching of the prophets. This first formation either actually is, or is represented by, what we call Deuteronomy. It was of course a compromise and included cultus as an ethical duty, which is not the true prophetic teaching. But it did include the

---

[23] Genesis 18:17–19.
[24] See H. E. Ryle, *The Canon of the Old Testament*, p. 69.

general prophetic theory that God's main requirement
for men is that each should treat others justly, and it
endeavored to give concrete explanation of what
"justly" means.[25]

A code of law was given,[26] and a blessing was pronounced on
obedience and a curse on disobedience.[27] Judah in 597 B.C. fell
before the Babylonian forces, and the exile supervened. Through
contact with other peoples there had developed a belief in God
as a holy God, who had chosen Israel to be His people. Because
the history of the nation was rewritten to show this fact, we have
the editorial process—the work of J, E, P, D, and R.

With the promulgation of Deuteronomy begins a new period
in the religion of Israel. That religion now had a book which
showed legal morality.[28] The D editors carried the work of the
authors of Deuteronomy to its logical conclusion, while the P
code gave directions for the proper preservation of the cult, a
means to preserve the holiness required of Israel by God.

THE P MATERIAL

P is later than D, for D shows no acquaintance with the
characteristic ideas or the ritual institutions of P, but draws
entirely on JE. The compilation of the Priestly Laws came about
because with the Babylonian destruction of the Temple in Jerusalem the religious ceremonies were in peril of being forgotten.
These Priestly Laws were compiled in Babylon, and with them
were combined the J and E narrative and the Deuteronomic
writings. R, or the work of the redactors, started with the Babylonian Exile.

P depends upon JE where he is dealing with persons or
places. P's is a priestly code written in the interests of the
priestly class. P protected Judaism from being disintegrated by
the influences of foreign culture, especially Hellenistic culture.

---

25 Kirsopp Lake, *Paul, His Heritage and Legacy,* p. 28.
26 Deuteronomy 12–26.
27 Deuteronomy 28:1–46.
28 Deuteronomy 7:6 ff.; 10:12–13.

All critics agree that the home of P was in Babylonia and "that the Priestly writer was one of the Jews that remained in Babylonia after 538, when many of the exiles returned." [29] The date is approximately 500 B.C.

The Priestly code is described as a book of four covenants or as four divisions of history: (1) from Adam to Noah; (2) from Noah to Abraham; (3) from Abraham to Moses; (4) from Moses to Joshua. The Priestly codex is important because the entire discussion of the Old Testament has turned upon its data.

P displays incongruities when injected into the old legends, for he tells us that Sarah at sixty-five is a beautiful woman whom the Egyptians seek to capture and that Ishmael at the age of sixteen is carried on his mother's shoulder. P gives the stories of creation, the deluge, God's appearance to Abraham, and the purchase of the cave at Machpelah. Everything else in P is detail and genealogy. With P, storytelling has ceased and his are mere facts and negotiations. We feel that P's style came about by his constant writing of contracts. The style of P is peculiar in its detailed, legal clearness. It is minute, precise and grows monotonous with its genealogies, its set phrases, and its outlines which lack substance. We see from the following short excerpts that P's story is legalistic, precise, formal:

> And Shem lived after he begat Arphaxad five hundred years, and begat sons and daughters.[30]
>
> And the field of Ephron, which was in Machpelah, which was before Mamre, the field, and the cave which was therein, and all the trees that were in the field, that were in all the borders round about, were made sure unto Abraham for a possession in the presence of the children of Heth, before all that went in at the gate of his city.[31]

P's style is dry because he deals with facts and presents them in outline form. His attitude is somewhat similar to his style,

---

[29] Brightman, *op. cit.*, p. 208.
[30] Genesis 11:11.
[31] Genesis 23:17,18.

because his regard for religion is objective rather than subjective. He does not speak of the personal piety of the patriarchs. P's dominant idea is that God created the world in order that His ordinances and commandments might be observed.

P's conception of God is transcendent, loftier and more advanced than that of the old legends, and less anthropomorphic than E's. P excludes all holy places except the Temple, and also excludes all the sacred springs and trees. P's motivating idea is found in form and ceremonies and in blind obedience. P is more interested in correct deportment than in inner righteousness. P says that Isaac's blessing of Jacob is a result of Esau's mixed marriages.

> And Esau was forty years old when he took to wife Judith the daughter of Beeri the Hittite, and Bathemath the daughter of Elon the Hittite: which were a grief of mind unto Isaac and Rebekah.[32]
> And Isaac called Jacob, and blessed him, and charged him, and said unto him, Thou shalt not take a wife of the daughters of Canaan.[33]

P purified the religion of the patriarchs and purged their morality. He omits altogether all that is offensive: Lot's selfishness, Jacob's deception, the exile of Ishmael. P's is the voice of the priest who feels that the worship at the Temple in Jerusalem is the only legitimate worship and is the continuation of the worship instituted by Moses. Judah recognized that her fathers had sinned and that a reformation was necessary. When the priesthood was restored, Judah was under the dominion of the priests.

A renaissance must have taken place between the time of J and E and the time of P, a renaissance which created something new in the place of the old nationality represented in the legends. P is considered a genuine author by some critics, while J and E are called collectors.[34] Other critics say that P is not

---

[32] Genesis 26:34,35.
[33] Genesis 28:1.
[34] Gunkel, *op. cit.*, p. 153.

written by one author at one time but that P is like a law book
that has been amended by successive sessions of a legislature.

Practically all critics since Wellhausen and Kuenen
distinguish at least four separate strata in P. They call
PH or H, the Code of Holiness. All critics agree that P
begins with the creation in Genesis I and extends
through the conquest of Canaan in Joshua.[35]

Because the legends from the time of Exodus have to do
chiefly with Moses, it was easy to combine both legends and
laws in one single book.

Remember ye the law of Moses my servant, which I
commanded unto him in Horeb for all Israel, with the
statutes and judgments. . . .[36]
Blessed are the undefiled in the way, who walk in
the law of the Lord.[37]
Open thou mine eyes, that I may behold wondrous
things out of thy law. . . .[38]
Give me understanding, that I shall keep thy law;
yea, I shall observe it with my whole heart.[39]

These citations show that the Law was the accredited standard
of doctrine for all Israel, and also show the high esteem in which
it was held. Even in the New Testament—

Jesus answered them, Is it not written in your law . . . ? [40]
In the law it is written, With men of other tongues
and other lips will I speak unto this people; and yet
for all that will they not hear me, saith the Lord.[41]

The Law represents the final stage in the long process of
compilation, though the Law (the Pentateuch) is traditionally

---

[35] Brightman, *op. cit.*, p. 203; also read Leviticus 17–26.
[36] Malachi 4:4.
[37] Psalms 119:1.
[38] Psalms 119:18.
[39] Psalms 119:34.
[40] John 10:34.
[41] I Corinthians 14:21.

ascribed to Mosaic authorship. Moses was the first leader to give Israel legislation. Subsequent laws in the course of Hebrew history, which were drawn up to meet changed conditions in Israel, were ascribed also to Moses. The Pentateuch (or the Law) embodies these codes of law; hence the Jews attributed the authorship of the first five books of the Old Testament to Moses.

> Just as later painters of great battles or other high ex-
> ploits of history fill their canvases with gorgeous color,
> so these writers of the Hebrew chronicles wove the
> purple of their interpretation into the threads of the old
> accounts which from generation to generation had been
> handed down. They saw the figure of Moses looming
> greater and greater against the mists of time. They tell
> of acts of his which may have had originally some sim-
> ple explanation in his knowledge of the region and in
> his own sagacity, but which they describe in amazing
> fashion as though they were the immediate miracles of
> God. And especially they exalt Moses as the supreme
> lawgiver of Israel, and attribute to him and to his voice
> as a spokesman direct from God the whole body of the
> moral and ceremonial law which doubtless came gradu-
> ally into being.[42]

That the whole body of moral and ceremonial law came gradually into being can be best shown by a few historical facts. At the time of the fall of Jerusalem, 586 B.C., the literature consisted of oral tradition, fragments of ancient writings, the lost book, and the three documents J, E, and D, as well as composites and revisions of these. There were also the teachings of the prophets up to that time, both oral and written. At the end of the Babylonian captivity there were, in addition to these mentioned, the P document, and whatever knowledge had been gained in Babylon. The influence of the Exile is shown in vocabulary and style.

If R is made to stand for the work of the redactors, the

---

[42] Walter Russell Bowie, *The Story of the Bible*, p. 101.

Torah, or the Law, in its final form may be symbolized as JEDPR. The welding together of these documents is significant of the Jewish spirit. That such independent writings, so divergent in style, thought and date, could have been pieced together into one organic whole is amazing, particularly when we can see for ourselves their mutually inconsistent facts set down beside each other with little attempt at harmonizing them.

The remainder of this chapter will show how these independent writings, J, E, D, and P, are welded together in Genesis, Exodus, Leviticus, Numbers, and Deuteronomy into one organic whole—the Jewish Law (Torah), or the Pentateuch.

GENESIS

The book of Genesis is divided into two parts. The first eleven chapters are given to us by P and J and offer a splendid contrast. The P document, the exilic work of the priests, is seen at its best in the sublime account of creation in the first chapter. The compilers perhaps used the P document first because they wished to turn the origin of the universe into a glorification of the Jewish Sabbath.

P's story of creation we find related in the first chapter of Genesis and in the first three verses of the second chapter:

> In the beginning God created the heaven and the earth. And the earth was without form, and void; and darkness was upon the face of the deep. And the Spirit of God moved upon the face of the waters. And God said, Let there be light: and there was light. . . . And God blessed the seventh day, and sanctified it: because that in it he had rested from all his work which God created and made.

This majestic story of creation which stands at the beginning of the Old Testament is late (as we showed in our discussion of the P document) as a literary composition. P gives us a series of conceptions rather than a picture. The idea of the Sabbath's being embedded in the creation is merely the expression of P's priestly purpose. These first eleven chapters deal with the traditions of the primeval world. In the second part of Genesis, from chapters 12 to 50, the E document tells us of the traditions of the Hebrew people.

> The stories of Genesis came from various sources. Some are the stories of local places; some are the traditions of tribes, told about the ancestral heroes. They had long been told orally before they were written down. Such popular stories soon take a certain literary form, usually known as the folk-tale form, which is marked by simplicity, directness, repetition, and often climax and humor. To call a story a folk tale is not to pass a judgment on its historical value, but only to classify it as literature. Folk stories, whether legend or history, formed the best material for religious teaching which an early race possessed. The teachers of many races have so used their ancient tales, but none have molded them into as rich a body of religious truth as have the writers of the early Hebrew books.
>
> In spite of the variety of sources, there is a unity of purpose in Genesis. God guiding the affairs of men and fulfilling His plan through them, is the main religious conception of the book.[43]

The second story of creation is J's story, beginning with the second chapter of Genesis, the fourth verse, to the fourth chapter. J describes God not as P described Him, as a lofty and distant Being, but as having human attributes. He experiments; He walks and talks with men; He discovers what has happened by inquiry; He is intimate, compassionate, companionable. There is no repetition, no formality of style; the story is picturesque rather than abstract, concrete rather than general. There are explanations of names on the basis of the resemblance of their sound to words in the current Hebrew of the writer's time—Adam (*ada-mah*, ground), Eve (*hava*, to live). The purpose of the story is found in the prophetic teaching that sin

---

[43] Wood and Grant, *The Bible as Literature*, p. 107.

brings suffering.[44] There is freedom of expression in the J document, as compared to the rigid formality of the P doctrine.

In the story of the flood we have the J and P documents interwoven rather than separate as we have in the story of creation. The P story is Genesis 6:9–22; 7:6,11,13–16,17–21,24; 8:1–2,3–5,14–19; 9:1–17,28,29 and a few phrases inserted into the J material by the editor. The remainder is J. The J account of the flood is picturesque and is not given in the narrow, restricted, abstract way in which P relates the story.

> And God saw that the wickedness of man was great in the earth, and that every imagination of the thoughts of his heart was only evil continually. And it repented the Lord that he had made man on the earth, and it grieved him at his heart. And the Lord said, I will destroy man whom I have created from the face of the earth; both man, and beast, and the creeping thing, and the fowls of the air; for it repenteth me that I have made them.[45]

J's story of the flood strengthens the idea that sin brings suffering but that repentance and righteousness bring the fellowship and blessing of God. J's God promises never to destroy the earth again. But P's God establishes a covenant with man. He is less anthropomorphic than J's God.

> P uses the same original story to lead up to a little code of law, given by the free grace of God to understanding man. Both purposes are religious, but with the characteristic differences.[46]

P's story follows in part:

> These are the generations of Noah: Noah was a just man and perfect in his generations, and Noah walked with God. And Noah begat three sons, Shem, Ham, and Japheth. The earth also was corrupt before God,

[44] Wood and Grant, *op. cit.*, p. 108.
[45] Genesis 6:5–7.
[46] Wood and Grant, *op. cit.*, p. 112.

and the earth was filled with violence. And God looked upon the earth, and, behold, it was corrupt; for all flesh had corrupted his way upon the earth.[47]

In Genesis 25:19–20 from the P document we find:

And these are the generations of Isaac, Abraham's son: Abraham begat Isaac: and Isaac was forty years old when he took Rebekah to wife, the daughter of Bethuel the Syrian of Padan-aram, the sister to Laban the Syrian.

These two verses are used as an introduction to the combined stories. Verse 20 is all that P has regarding Isaac's marriage. The rich narrative of chapter 24 makes us realize that this is from JE. In Genesis 25:26 we have a fragment from P telling of the birth of Esau and Jacob. Verses 27 and 28 of chapter 25 are an introduction to the story in chapter 27. These verses are from J with the exception of the words "a man of the field" and "dwelling in tents," which are fragments from the parallel E account. Genesis 25:29–34 is the story of Esau's selling Jacob his birthright and is from J. In Genesis 26:34–35, we have an account of Esau's marriages; this passage is from P.

Genesis 28:10–22 is the story of Jacob at Bethel and is also from J and E. Jacob comes to Bethel and by chance spends the night there, "and tarried there all night, because the sun was set; and he took the stones at that place, and put them for his pillows." Jacob dreamed that God's messengers were walking up and down a ladder set up from earth to heaven. Jacob, anointing the stone, inaugurates a custom of sanctuary; he also institutes tithe-giving. This is the concrete E version of the story, which is made up of early and late parts.

The J version has a different emphasis; the revelation of the holiness of the place is not the point of the story, but the promise made to Jacob by the God of his fathers. The concreteness of this story is in direct contrast to Genesis 12:8, which makes Abraham the founder of the sanctuary. This story implies that Bethel was always a Yahweh sanctuary.

---

[47] Genesis 6:9–12.

Genesis 29:15–30 gives us Jacob's marriage to Leah and Rachel and comes from J and E. Jacob, who has deceived his father and brother, now gets a taste of his own medicine from Laban.

In Genesis 30:25–43 we have Jacob's new agreement with Laban, which is from J and E. Genesis 31:1–16 is God's command to Jacob to return to his home; verses 1 and 3 are from J, but the rest of this passage is from E. E appears to be a trifle uneasy as to the morality of Jacob's methods; hence he gives a long speech in which Jacob sets forth his innocence. Laban's own daughters decide against their father. E is referring in this passage to the Bethel story, which brings unity to the cycle.

Genesis 32:3–24, Jacob's preparations for meeting with Esau, is from J and E. Jacob's meeting with Esau is a friendly one[48] and is given to us by J and E.[49]

In Genesis 37 we have the story of Joseph, who is sold into Egypt. According to the J version, the cause of his brothers' hatred for Joseph is the long garment with sleeves. When he finds his brothers at Shechem, it is Judah who prevents their killing him. They sell him to the Ishmaelites, and send his coat, dipped in blood, to Jacob. Joseph is taken to Egypt and sold to an Egyptian.

According to the E version, Joseph's dreams are the cause of the ill feeling. Reuben is his protector. Joseph is cast into a pit and found by the Midianites, who take him to Egypt and sell him to Potiphar.

According to the P version, Joseph's tale-bearing is the cause of the ill feelings. The rest of the story has been dropped in favor of the J and E versions.

In Genesis 40, Joseph interprets the dreams of the chief butler and of the chief baker of Pharaoh. From J come "that the butler of the king of Egypt and his baker had offended their lord the king of Egypt"[50] and "and here also have I done nothing that they should put me into the dungeon."[51] The rest is

---

[48] Genesis 33:1–6.
[49] For these detailed facts, I am indebted to E. S. Brightman, *The Sources of the Hexateuch*, pp. 32 ff.
[50] Genesis 40:1.
[51] Genesis 40:15.

E's version. According to the J version, Joseph is in prison. The
king of Egypt's butler and baker are confined in the same place.
The Pharaoh is called "king of Egypt," and he apparently has
only one butler and one baker. But in the E version, Joseph is
in the house of Potiphar, the captain of the guard. The chief of
the butlers and the chief of the bakers of Pharaoh are sent to
this house, pending a decision on their case. It is implied here
that Pharaoh has a much more elaborate establishment than J
suggests.

According to J, Joseph advises Pharaoh to appoint overseers,
to gather up all the food in Egypt, which is to be laid up in the
cities. The famine is to be confined to Egypt. In E's version
Joseph advises the appointment of one man who will gather the
fifth part of the grain and store it under Pharaoh's supervision.
The famine is to extend over the whole earth. Apart from these
minor differences, the two versions run parallel, and the analysis
is uncertain.

In dealing with the story of Joseph and his brethren in
Egypt, we find that in J only Joseph's sons are blessed. Possibly
Joseph originally received the blessing. Jacob is blind, yet guides
his hands so as to bless Ephraim, the younger, with his right
hand. The superiority of the tribe of Ephraim is thus explained.

In the E document, Jacob simply mentions Ephraim before
Manasseh. Only Joseph's sons are blessed, and Jacob is not
blind.

In the P document, Jacob lives for seventeen years after his
coming into Egypt. All of Jacob's sons receive a blessing; hence,
this obscures the final pre-eminence of Joseph of the J and E
narratives. The religious views of the Joseph story are those of
J and E. Through the story runs the idea of the pervading,
continuous power of God, whose plans advance despite the sins
of men. Joseph is a complex character, an ideal rather than a
type. He is the loving son, the forgiving brother, a man of fore-
sight, chaste and upright.

The Joseph story is our first short story, and we find that it
is an organized whole. E's is the oldest version of the story that
tells of the saving of Joseph's life. What knowledge of Egypt

that the story reveals could well have been obtained from merchants and soldiers. The story is told as a means of getting the Israelites into Egypt, that the historical story of the Exodus might be introduced.

EXODUS

Just as we found in Genesis, the Exodus narrative contains many contradictions. The simplest and therefore the earliest form of the tradition is J_1. This document seems to have been incorporated, in whole or in part, in the more elaborate narrative of J_2, which in turn is further elaborated by J_3 and possibly by J_4. The narrative seems to have been in the main based on the same tradition as J_2, though it diverges from it markedly at times. It, too, has been subjected to elaboration. P, as usual, has revised the tradition to make it fit his theories, and has ignored most of the incidents which make for the richness of the earlier document. The J_1 material in Exodus 1, seems to be "(7) And the children of Israel were fruitful, and increased abundantly, and multiplied, and waxed exceeding mighty. . . . (8) Now there arose up a new king over Egypt, which knew not Joseph. (9) And he said unto his people, Behold, the people . . . are more and mightier than we. (10) Come on, let us deal wisely with them. . . . (15) And the king of Egypt spake to the Hebrew midwives . . . (16) And he said . . ." (to the end of verse 20).

Into this narrative has been inserted another tale which tells how the Egyptians reduced the Israelites to forced labor. This is incompatible with the former story, for it implies that the Egyptians were more numerous than the Israelites; and further, it would be against their own interests for the Egyptians to kill off the males of their slaves.

The P material in Exodus 1 is 1–5, 7 (except "and multiplied and waxed mighty"), 13, and 14 (except "in mortar and in brick"). Verses 20 and 21 seem to be later, inserted by someone who was interested in the later fate of the midwives. Verse 22 is the transition to the story of the birth of Moses, evidently replacing that of J_1.

In Exodus 2:1–10, the story of the birth of Moses, the J_1 material appears to be limited to verse 1. The tradition of Moses' semi-Egyptian origin was too strong to be altogether ignored, but the growing nationalism would not accept the Egyptian as his mother, hence the device of adoption. In Exodus 2:2–10, in the E version, we find that Moses is adopted by Pharaoh's daughter. In Exodus 2:11–15 the story of Moses' slaying the Egyptian seems to be from J_1. Exodus 2:21,22 also seem to be from J_1.

In summarizing, we may say that Moses' name, which is Egyptian, appears to indicate some connection with Egypt. His journey to Midian reflects the conviction of the writers of the story that the God in whose name he led the people from Egypt was connected with Midian. (Mount Sinai is in that region.) The story of the bulrushes, commentators agree, is a variant of a well-known folk tale. The story of the killing of the Egyptian is told to account for Moses' flight which brought him to Midian. The conclusion of the narrative has given place to the versions of J_2 and E. According to this narrative, Moses is told to return to Egypt. On the way he happens to stop at a holy place and is attacked. He is then given his commission to lead his people out of Egypt. The naïve representation of Egypt and the court is characteristic of J_1. An interesting fact is that of Pharaoh's reply in Exodus 5:2, "Who is Yahweh?" carrying the implications of a recently revealed name, still unknown to Pharaoh.

The narrative of the plagues[52] is composed of material from J, E, and P, and there are many signs of editing. The P narrative is as follows: Moses receives the command and transmits it to Aaron, who executes it with his rod. The magicians of Egypt attempt to reproduce the phenomenon, at first with success, then impotently. But the heart of Pharaoh is strong, and he will not listen.

> And Moses and Aaron did so, as the Lord commanded; and he lifted up the rod, and smote the waters that were in the river, in the sight of Pharaoh, and in

---

[52] Exodus 7:1 ff.; 10:28; 11:1 ff.

the sight of all his servants; and all the waters that
were in the river were turned to blood.[53]

P then shows the turning of the rod into a serpent, the turning
of all the water in Egypt into blood, the plague of frogs, followed in turn by the plague of lice and the plague of boils.

In the E document the people are living among the Egyptians. Moses stretches out his hand, with the rod, to bring the
plague. He makes no announcement of his intention to Pharaoh,
and Aaron enacts no part; yet act follows upon act. E then has
the turning of the water of the Nile, "and they shall be turned
to blood."[54] This plague is followed by the plague of hail, the
plague of locusts, and the plague of darkness.

In the J document the Israelites are in Goshen. Before each
plague Moses demands leave for the people to depart. The
plague is wrought by Yahweh, yet the heart of Pharaoh is hard-
ened. Time elapses between each of the ten plagues, but in the
J document Aaron takes no part as he does in the E document.
"Thus saith the lord . . . I will smite . . . upon the waters which
are in the river."[55] J has the plague of the fouling of the Nile
followed by the plague of the frogs, the plague of the flies,
the plague of murrain, the plague of hail, the plague of locusts.
There are, of course, redactional sentences.

In the study of Genesis and Exodus we have shown that J
furnished the greatest amount of material in Genesis, that J was
the oldest of the documents, and that his conception of Jehovah
was primitive and anthropomorphic. We showed that E's conception of Jehovah was less anthropomorphic than J's and that
E was interested in the shrines of the Northern Kingdom because E was written, in 750 B.C., in the Northern Kingdom. We
showed that the P document was compiled in Babylonia during
the Exile in the interest of the priestly class, and that the entire
discussion of the Old Testament was influenced by this document, for it was revised to fit his own theories. That these docu-

[53] Exodus 7:20.
[54] Exodus 7:17.
[55] Exodus 7:17.

ments were either interwoven or placed side by side accounts
for the repetition and the many contradictions in Genesis and
Exodus.

DEUTERONOMY

In Exodus 34:7 there is a blessing on those who keep the
commandments, "keeping mercy for thousands." In Exodus
20:12 and Deuteronomy 5:16 we have a blessing on those who
respect their parents, as against the curse in Deuteronomy 27:16.
We may postulate from this story the existence of a blessing and
a cursing ceremony at Shechem, the origin of which was
ascribed by Israelite tradition to a command of Moses. The
story of the command is used as a framework for the Deuteronomy code.

In Deuteronomy there is a law code demanding the regula-
tion of the whole life and religion of the nation. The D editors
believed that they were giving to the people the great principles
of the religion of Moses: the principle of the unity of God; the
principle of a single sanctuary; and social morality and worship
in accord with the purified sacrificial system. The Book of
Deuteronomy could not be published when it was written 650
B.C., but Manasseh's long, cruel reign was followed (with a
lapse of one year) by Josiah's reign. The time was auspicious for
the prophetic party during Josiah's reign, and in 621 B.C. Deuteronomy was published. This book was a recodification of Jewish
law, and was probably prepared during the suppression of the
prophets in the tyrannical reign of Manasseh. In Deuteronomy,
a movement or a reformation began, and the reformers apparently gained their ends.

The redactional work which we have discussed in three of
the five books of the Law—namely, Genesis, Exodus, and Deuteronomy—was formed by the weaving together of the various
expositions of Mosaic Law[56] and combining these with the
Jahwist and Elohist documents. In other words, the Jewish Law
(Genesis, Exodus, Leviticus, Numbers, and Deuteronomy) was

---

[56] Exodus 20–23, Deuteronomy, Leviticus 17–26, and the Priestly code.

formulated by the weaving together of the various documents J, E, D, P. Historical facts have been presented when necessary to clarify the formation of the first canon, the Law (the Torah, or our Pentateuch). It has been necessary, occasionally, to present facts in this chapter which deal with the Priestly Law or with Ezra and Nehemiah. These facts would seem, at first thought, to belong to the material in Chapter Three, The Writings. However, the Priestly code, or P, was written during the Exile, and the canonization of the Law took place about 444 B.C.

We ask, then, why the P document was written, and under whom was the Law made canonical. In Babylon, expatriation had filled the priests with a burning desire to write out their hereditary usages, which when written formed the document P, or the Priestly code. Ezra, the scribe, in 457 B.C. and Nehemiah in 444 B.C. were sent from Babylon with help for the Jerusalem Jews, and under these two leaders the Law was made canonical.[57]

> The modern critical school ascribes to Ezra, not merely the enforcement, but the redaction and even the authorship of a substantial portion of what subsequently became known as the Torah—the Law of Moses. . . . With Ezra, the reign of the Torah over the Jewish people began. . . . Houses of prayer were now set up, perhaps for the first time, in localities distant from the Temple; a practice encouraged by the exigencies of the Babylonian Exile. In them, the Torah was not only read, but also expounded.[58]

The leading critics of the nineteenth century agreed

> . . . that all the sources into which they divided the Pentateuch were older than the Babylonian exile, and the prevailing opinion was that they had been united in the composite whole as we now have it in the gen-

---

[57] Nehemiah 8–10.
[58] From *A Bird's-Eye View of Jewish History,* by Cecil Roth (Union of American Hebrew Congregations, 1935), p. 67.

eration between the introduction of Deuteronomy (621) and the fall of Jerusalem (586), or that, at the latest, it was completed in Babylonia in the following generation. They agreed also that the source which begins in Genesis I and includes the bulk of the legislation in Exodus, Leviticus and Numbers, though not all of the same origin or age, was the oldest stratum of narrative and law in the Pentateuch, and Deuteronomy the latest. Ezra was, as in the traditional view, the restorer of the law. He brought up the Pentateuch from Babylonia; and was chiefly instrumental in getting it put in force as the law of the returned exiles in Judæa.[59]

The Law (Torah), or our Pentateuch, was completed about 444 B.C. and was divided for convenience into five books, Genesis, Exodus, Leviticus, Numbers, and Deuteronomy.

The principle of canonization was divine inspiration; i.e., these books were regarded as sacred, because they contained the word of God; and as such they were the final authority, the fundamental law of the Jewish community. Moses had been merely God's spokesman, His mouthpiece, nothing else; the real author was God. There had been several stages in the process of canonization; the most notable was the adoption of the Deuteronomic law at the time of Josiah's reformation and the recognition of the Priest code at the time of Ezra. When all the various laws together with the narratives belonging to the sources of which they formed a part were combined—the Torah of Moses—the Pentateuch was complete, the canon of the law was perfect. It has remained the highest Jewish authority ever since.[60]

---

[59] Reprinted by permission of the publishers from George Foot Moore's *Judaism in the First Centuries of the Christian Era* (Cambridge, Mass.: Harvard University Press, 1927), Vol. I, pp. 9–10.

[60] J. A. Bewer, *The Literature of the Old Testament in Its Historical Development*, p. 427.

• II •

The Prophets

We found that the first canon, the Law, dealt with the origin of the Hebrew race and with the foundation of the Israelite religion. But the Law lacked the element of prophecy. The Law (the Torah) did not represent the fullness or the freedom of prophecy. This freedom was felt and expressed through the literary activity of the Jews of Babylon during and after the Exile. The Book of Joshua, based on the narratives of J and E, was compiled during the Exile, and was edited in the spirit of the Deuteronomic law. Joshua and Deuteronomy are alike in style and subject matter, but an interval elapsed between the canonization of the Law and the final acceptance of Joshua.

The old Hebrew tradition divided the canon of the Prophets into two sections. The Former Prophets included the books of Joshua, Judges, I and II Samuel, and I and II Kings; and the Latter Prophets consisted of material grouped into four sections, Isaiah, Jeremiah, Ezekiel, and the twelve Minor Prophets: Hosea, Joel, Amos, Obadiah, Jonah, Micah, Nahum, Habakkuk, Zephaniah, Haggai, Zechariah, and Malachi. Because the work of Isaiah, Jeremiah, and Ezekiel bulked larger than the pamphlets of Amos or Hosea, they were given first position as major prophets.

In reality, the so-called Former Prophets represent the history books of the ancient Hebrews and are also known as "the prophetic histories," because the influence of the prophets furnished the stimulus to gather and compile them. They were associated with the prophetic writings under the mistaken supposition that they had been written by certain of the prophets. Of course, prophetic teaching had a great deal to do with the molding and the shaping of the national history, and in that sense it is not difficult to understand why these books joined hands with the various collections of sermons by the prophets.

There was no love lost between priest and prophet at any time, but as a rule the earlier prophets prescribed nothing more than some relatively unimportant variation of the ideas of the priests.

> One after the other, men such as Amos, Hosea, Micah, and Isaiah arose in rapid succession, and in the most violent language denounced the whole apparatus of the priesthood. Like their predecessors, they claimed inspiration for their message, but the message was wholly different. God, they said, does not care for presents or compliments. He merely wishes men to behave well to one another. God does not want sacrifices; He does not want services of devotion and praise, and He does not desire to hear prayers, except from those who have qualified by their treatment of men to have the privilege of addressing God.[1]

The prophets, though often suffering persecution, were always honored by the Jewish nation, and were considered more divinely inspired than any other of their great men except Moses. These prophets became very prominent first in the history of the Northern Kingdom. Elijah denounced the wicked King Ahab as early as the latter part of the ninth century B.C. Elijah was followed by Elisha, Amos, and Hosea in the Northern

---

[1] Kirsopp Lake, *Paul, His Heritage and Legacy*, pp. 25–26.

Kingdom. Six prophets belong to the Assyrian period: Amos and Hosea in the Northern Kingdom, about the middle of the eighth century B.C., and Isaiah and Micah in the Southern Kingdom, a little later, while Zephaniah and Nahum belong to the early part of the seventh century B.C. Jeremiah and Habakkuk were pre-exilic prophets of the Chaldean period, and Ezekiel prophesied during the former part of the Captivity.

About two hundred years after the Law was canonized, there came over the Jewish people an intense desire to preserve the words of the prophets; hence around the year 200 B.C. these various prophetic documents were collected into a single volume. These prophetic books were not arranged in the order of their historical sequence. The men who planned this classification were not especially concerned with chronological problems or with the question of correct dates. What interested them was the greatness of the message. It was only natural that the completed volumes began to take on a certain degree of holiness, which grew from year to year until, by popular esteem and veneration, the Prophets came to be regarded as sacred literature, second only to the Law. The Jews were willing to admit the Prophets beside the Law as a part of their divinely inspired literature. The canon of the Prophets, like that of the Law, is a compilation.

Before we discuss the compilation of a few of the individual books constituting the second canon, or the Prophets, we shall review, briefly, the historical facts necessary to the understanding of this compilation. First, let us ask ourselves, What brought about the first translation of the Hebrew Bible into Greek? This came about because of the great number of Jews who went to Alexandria (founded in 332 B.C.) rather than return, after the Exile, to Jerusalem.

In the third century B.C., the proportion of Greek-speaking Jews became so great that it was necessary to translate the Hebrew Bible into Greek, and between 280 and 130 B.C. this translation was made. It is called the Septuagint (LXX) because tradition tells us that it was translated by seventy or seventy-two men. These translators rearranged the book in what they considered a better order, and included certain books, called the Apocrypha, which had not been included in the Hebrew canon. This Greek Bible was later translated into Latin as the Vulgate. The order of the Septuagint is contrasted in this chapter with the order of the Hebrew Bible.

The next question that we shall discuss is the fusion of the different elements of Israel and Canaan. In considering the fusion of these elements it is important to remember the difference between cultural levels. Canaan had a cultural background of its own. The Canaanites had walled towns and were different in the tone of their lives, which involved community living. Archaeologists have revealed the culture of the land in excavations and have made it clear that there is no real break in the continuity of culture in the land of Canaan. The coming of Israel into Canaan could not mean a leveling of old culture and a beginning of new, for the nomads were absorbed into the culture of the land into which they came. Jahwism was enormously modified, but alone preserved its identity. Baal was pre-eminently a local divinity exercising supreme power within a local area.

Gideon was told to cut down the altar of Baal and to build an altar to God. The Canaanites who occupied the land worshipped the Baalim, local gods who were supposed to control the sources of fertility. When Israel first came into Canaan the opposition between Jahweh and Canaan was felt. But when the initial struggle was over an equilibrium was reached, and there came about a gradual fusion which resulted in intermarriage. Marriage naturally demanded that both religions be taken account of. At critical times, Jahweh was looked to for help, but in normal times the prevailing religion was accepted.

Israel learned to cultivate the land, and so gave some recognition to the gods of the land. Necessity of trade between the two elements made them recognize other gods, yet made them call God to witness. There was a necessity of arriving at an arrangement between the two religions, but there was also a tendency for Jahwism to be assimilated to the prevailing religion.

THE BOOK OF JUDGES

The Book of Judges[2] recognized this assimilation's taking place. We have shown that intermarriage involved accepting the worship of the land of Canaan. Disregard of Jahweh, the Old Testament teaches, always leads to decline in prosperity of the people. In the subjection of the Canaanites, the Israelites came to realize Jahweh's place and power. The theory of the Book of Judges is found in this passage:

> And the children of Israel did evil again in the sight of the Lord, and served Baalim, and Ashtaroth, and the gods of Syria, and the gods of Zidon, and the gods of Moab, and the gods of the children of Ammon, and the gods of the Philistines, and forsook the Lord, and served not him. . . . Nevertheless the Lord raised up judges, which delivered them out of the hand of those that spoiled them.[3]

Israel was tempted to be assimilated in the land, but wars preserved her. It was Jahweh, however, who lifted up the children of Israel and delivered them, for we are told that "the spirit of the Lord came upon Jephthah."[4]

The Book of Judges covers four centuries, and the material presented is limited to that length of time. The material needed much manipulation to make it cover the period. The editors were trying to make the local incidents national in character. They were trying to write the history of the land as a whole, just as they considered that the nation came into Canaan as a unit. Throughout Judges, Jahweh is pre-eminently the War God, and it is this constant fighting that preserves Israel from being absorbed in the land of Canaan. Through the power of Jahweh, the Judges did mighty things.

---

[2] Comments and information on Judges, I and II Samuel, and I and II Kings have come from Professor S. F. Pattison's course, *The Bible as Literature*, University of Arizona; from J. A. Bewer, *The Literature of the Old Testament in Its Historical Development;* from James Hastings, *Dictionary of the Bible.*

[3] Judges 10:6.

[4] Judges 11:29.

The Deuteronomic editors have worked out, in the Book of Judges, a philosophy of history—a period of well-being when they have been loyal, a period of evil days when they have forsaken their religion. The Israelites took the land from the Canaanites, and when they were settled and the fusion had taken place, God led them in defending the land from invaders. These deeds arose from the power and presence of Jahweh, as is seen in the cases of Gideon and Deborah:

> And the angel of the Lord appeared unto him, and said unto him, The Lord is with thee, thou mighty man of valour. And Gideon said unto him, Oh my Lord, if the Lord be with us, why then is all this befallen us? and where be all his miracles which our fathers told us of, saying, Did not the Lord bring us up from Egypt? but now the Lord hath forsaken us, and delivered us into the hands of the Midianites. And the Lord looked upon him, and said, Go in this thy might, and thou shalt save Israel from the hand of the Midianites.[5]

> And the Lord said unto Gideon, By the three hundred men that lapped will I save you, and deliver the Midianites into thine hand.[6]

In the song of Deborah and Barak we have one of the greatest of war songs:

> Praise ye the Lord
> For the avenging of Israel,
> When the people willingly offered themselves.
> Hear, O ye kings; give ear, O ye princes;
> I, even I, will sing unto the Lord;
> I will sing praise to the Lord God of Israel.
>
> .   .   .   .
>
> My heart is toward the governors of Israel,
> That offered themselves willingly among the people.

---

[5] Judges 6:12–14.
[6] Judges 7:7.

Bless ye the Lord.

.   .   .   .

Awake, awake, Deborah:
Awake, awake, utter a song:
Arise, Barak, and lead thy captivity captive, thou son
    of Abinoam.
Then he made him that remaineth have dominion
    over the nobles among the people:
The Lord made me have dominion over the mighty.[7]

The Samson stories we find in Judges 14–16. In Judges 15:20
we are told that "he judged Israel in the days of the Philistines
twenty years," which is the formula usually concluding the
stories of Judges. This suggests that some earlier editor's account
came to conclusion there. Some later editor may have added the
sixteenth chapter. There is a rough parallelism in the fourteenth,
fifteenth, and sixteenth chapters.

The account of the birth of Samson is religious in its intention,[8] yet chapters 14 and 15 are similar in character, except
with reference to Jahweh.

And Sampson called upon the Lord, and said, O Lord
God, remember me, I pray thee, and strengthen me,
I pray thee, only this once, O God, that I may be at
once avenged of the Philistines for my two eyes.[9]

We can easily see that the Books of Samuel should immediately follow the Samson stories in Judges, for these stories give
the background struggles with the Philistines. However, the
Septuagint inserted the charming story of Ruth between Judges
and I Samuel, because the story is said to have happened in the
days of the judges. The Hebrew order is different and truer to
the chronological order, for the Pentateuch is followed by the
four historical books of the Prophets: Joshua, Judges, I and II
Samuel, and I and II Kings.

---

[7] Judges 5:2–13.
[8] Judges 13:24.
[9] Judges 16:28.

I AND II SAMUEL

The books of Samuel are a compilation which contains ancient elements. The work of compilation may have taken place during the exilic period. In I and II Samuel, the composite character is expressed:

> And the rest of the acts of Solomon, and all that he did, and his wisdom, are they not written in the book of the acts of Solomon?[10]

There are also in Kings clearly marked excerpts from a narrative history of the prophets.

> And they answered him, He was an hairy man, and girt with a girdle of leather about his loins. And he said, It is Elijah the Tishbite.[11]

This compilation is placed by critics at the close of the sixth century B.C.

Before the Exile, the prophets found themselves in opposition to the prevailing form of religion in Israel. Toward the close of the Exile, their prestige was enhanced by the fulfilment of the predictions of Jeremiah. The mission of the prophets was firmly established, and the people were determined to preserve their words.

Let us consider a few of the geographical and historical facts which will make the study of I and II Samuel clearer. The original home of the Philistines was Caphtor,[12] the coast of the Egyptian delta. At the beginning of the twelfth century, there was a southward movement in Palestine. Close to the time of the Exodus, however, the cities occupied were Gaza, the point at which the trade routes separate, one into Egypt, the other to the Gulf of Akabah, Ashdod, Eglon,[13] and Ascalon.

Palestine was the land of the Philistines, and the struggle with the Philistines gradually brought about the formation of

---

[10] I Kings 11:41.
[11] II Kings 1:8.
[12] See Deuteronomy 2:23 and Amos 9:7.
[13] See Joshua 10:36; 12:12; 15:39.

the kingdom of Israel. This formation had been attempted previously under Abimelech, but was unsuccessful. There was no antagonism between the two peoples after the actual forming of the kingdom. The leader in this formation was Saul. The books are called I and II Samuel because the leading character of I Samuel is Samuel. The outstanding figure, though, is Saul.

In I Samuel 9–10, we find that Saul was anointed king by Samuel, "the anointed of Jahweh." This story is to show the power of Jahweh in Saul, who was the ruler at a time of great distress. Because of his personality, the people rallied about him.

In the first part of the book, however, Samuel is the hero. He became judge and ruler over all Israel. The Philistines were under his leadership. Upon close examination, we find a later period following this period in the part Saul played in Israel: Saul's rash, impulsive leadership, his obstinacy, his stubbornness. I Samuel 14 favors Jonathan, but portrays Saul as a royal leader, in complete control, for he has organized the northern tribes into a unity.

In the defiance of Israel by Goliath, we find that David is first brought into prominence:

> And Saul and the men of Israel were gathered together, and pitched by the valley of Elah, and set the battle in array against the Philistines. And the Philistines stood on a mountain on the one side, and Israel stood on a mountain on the other side: and there was a valley between them.
>
> And there went out a champion out of the camp of the Philistines, named Goliath. . . . And he stood and cried unto the armies of Israel, and said unto them, Why are ye come out to set your battle in array? am not I a Philistine, and ye servants to Saul? choose you a man for you, and let him come down to me. If he be able to fight with me, and to kill me, then will we be your servants: but if I prevail against him, and kill him, then shall ye be our servants, and serve us. . . .

And David said to Saul, Let no man's heart fail because of him; thy servant will go and fight with this Philistine. And Saul said to David, Thou art not able to go against this Philistine to fight with him: for thou art but a youth, and he a man of war from his youth. . . .

Then said David to the Philistine, Thou comest to me with a sword, and with a spear, and with a shield: but I come to thee in the name of the Lord of hosts, the God of the armies of Israel, whom thou has defied. . . .

And as David returned from the slaughter of the Philistine, Abner took him, and brought him before Saul with the head of the Philistine in his hand.[14]

This chapter shows that victory came not through the resources of Israel but through God. It also dramatizes the struggle and goes to the heart of the religious significance of the God of the armies of Israel.

We are interested in the earliest form or document of the rise of David.

. . . and when Saul saw any strong man, or any valiant man, he took him unto him.[15]

Then answered one of the servants, and said, Behold, I have seen a son of Jesse the Beth-lehemite, that is cunning in playing, and a mighty valiant man, and a man of war, and prudent in matters, and a comely person, and the Lord is with him. . . . And David came to Saul, and stood before him: and he loved him greatly; and he became his armourbearer.[16]

And the women answered one another as they played, and said, Saul hath slain his thousands, and David his ten thousands. And Saul was very wroth, and

---

14 I Samuel 17:2–4,8–9,32–33,45,57.
15 I Samuel 14:52.
16 I Samuel 16:18,21

the saying displeased him. . . . And Saul eyed David from that day forward.[17]

And Michal Saul's daughter loved David: and they told Saul, and the thing pleased him. And Saul said, I will give him her, that she may be a snare to him, and that the hand of the Philistines may be against him.[18] [An earlier story.]

Saul also sent messengers unto David's house, to watch him, and to slay him in the morning.[19]

And David arose, and fled that day for fear of Saul, and went to Achish the king of Gath.[20] [This narrative of David is getting nearer to fact.]

David therefore departed thence, and escaped to the cave Adullam.[21]

In I Samuel 22:6–23 we are told of David's wanderings and dangers, and we note that these verses show a different editorship from the factual verses of chapter 21. I Samuel 24 and 26 tell us of David's magnanimity to Saul. There is no certainty as to which is the earliest version, but critics are inclined to believe that chapter 24 is the earlier. These stories all shed light upon the way people felt toward David, but they were told after David had become great and gave to him a heroic characterization. We do not get Saul's side of the story.

In chapters 29 and 30 of I Samuel we are told of the resumption of war between the Philistines and Israel. These two narratives are interwoven. In 29:2 one narrative speaks of the "lords of the Philistines," while in verse 3 a second narrative speaks of "the princes of the Philistines." It is difficult to determine which is the earlier of these two narratives.

Chapter 31 closes I Samuel with the final struggle and death of Saul. In the earlier narratives there was a breach between

---

[17] I Samuel 18:7–9.
[18] I Samuel 18:20–21.
[19] I Samuel 19:11.
[20] I Samuel 21:10.
[21] I Samuel 22:1.

Saul and the priesthood. This later tradition is probably a reflection of the first breach. II Samuel, chapter 1, is a second account of Saul's death and is different from the first account, in which Saul kills himself.

In II Samuel, chapter 6, the Ark story is more historical than the Ark story in I Samuel 5. In II Samuel, we are told that the Ark was brought to Jerusalem to establish it as the capital of entire Israel. In capturing Jerusalem, David established it as his capital. The Ark symbolized Jahweh's presence. Legends identify the Ark with the sanctuary at Shiloh, which was used in the wars against Shiloh. Other traditions associate it with desert wanderings, and have it made under the direction of Moses. In Numbers 10:35, the Ark was associated with Jahweh as Israel's God of War.

In II Samuel 8 an early editor brings to a close his account of David's reign by giving a summary account of his accomplishments. In I Chronicles 18:1–17, this same material is used by the priestly editors, yet much which is not to David's credit is left out by these priestly editors.

In these historical narratives we have many legends and myths, and much romance, yet of no other people in the world have we the complete history that we have of Israel. There is an orderly sequence of events, and these editors knew how to write and how to make their characters live. They reveal the feelings of their characters objectively. We see that David sins, yet he is a son of God. David accepts his punishment and shows what repentance is. He gives Jahweh's will full control over his life. Each writer is charged with a sense of God's working through the individual for the fulfilment of His will. God's will was worked out nationally, a sense of the pervasive presence of Jahweh in the world.

David is the outstanding man of Israel after Moses. He is the founder of the nation. He is a statesman, a military leader, a builder, a man who was impressive, loyal to friend and foe, magnanimous, sensitive to women's beauty, yet deeply religious, brave and chivalrous.

I AND II KINGS

The editors of I and II Kings are not attempting to give a complete history in these books but are giving the most important events. The rest of the record is given by the priestly code in I and II Chronicles.

> And Nadab the son of Jeroboam began to reign over Israel in the second year of Asa king of Judah, and reigned over Israel two years. And he did evil in the sight of the Lord, and walked in the way of his father, and in his sin wherewith he made Israel to sin.[22]

I Kings 1–11 deals with the reign of Solomon. It was a peaceable reign until the close, and the Deuteronomy editors feel that toward the close of his life Solomon was under the influence of his foreign wives and served other gods. The Old Testament people were sure that God made his will known in dreams: "And Solomon awoke; and, behold, it was a dream."[23]

The kingdom of Solomon takes its place in an international setting. He makes treaties with tribes; he has a definite relationship with Tyre; and his kingdom is a commercial center. Solomon built a high place to the God of Moab, for it was necessary to make provision for foreign wives that they might worship their own gods.[24] This was dangerous, for the loyalty to Jahweh had laid hold on the lives of the people of Israel. Israel was on its way to become one of the great powers of the ancient world.

In I Kings, chapter 12, we have not just history but the dramatization of what actually took place. Rehoboam went to Shechem to be crowned king of the Northern Kingdom. "Israel" was the name given to the Northern Kingdom, while "Judah" was the name given to the Southern Kingdom.

It seems to be the formula that the kings of the Northern Kingdom were always made to do evil, and to make Israel sin.

---

[22] I Kings 15:25–26.
[23] I Kings 3:15.
[24] I Kings 11:7.

Omri brought order into the Northern Kingdom, for he founded the first substantial dynasty. Ahab was the son and successor of Omri. It is unfair to regard him as a wicked king, but he was guided by political rather than by religious considerations. He checked the advance of Damascus and Assyria. He retained, through half of his reign, control over Moab. He was married to Jezebel, the daughter of Ethbaal, king of Tyre. She had been a priestess herself in Sidon, and for her he built a sanctuary to her god, but he did not regard this act as hostile to Yahweh. However, to Elijah, Ahab's conduct was reprehensible.

From about 900 B.C. for about two and one-half centuries Assyria was the dominant power of the ancient world. Damascus and Israel were united probably because of the threat of Assyrian advance. The following excerpt will show clearly the history of the Northern and Southern Kingdoms.

> When from a precarious hold and a divided tribal existence the Hebrews, now called Israel, passed to political union they became a monarchy under Saul, David, and Solomon. These three reigns illustrate very well the rise, climax and decay of a petty kingdom. After the death of Solomon the kingdom split into two. The house of David continued to rule in the southern kingdom which was called Judah, while a rival series of dynasties ruled in the northern kingdom of Israel. The northern kingdom was the richer but also the more turbulent and came to an end one hundred and thirty-five years earlier than the other.[25]

Saul began to reign in 1025 B.C., but hardly had Saul seated himself on the throne when Yahweh rejected him, and bid Samuel anoint David to succeed him.[26] David reigned from 1010 to 970 B.C., when Solomon, his son, came to the throne. The date given for the division into Northern and Southern Kingdoms is 932 B.C. The north had resources and power but no strong leaders; hence there were many rulers during this period.

---

[25] Wood and Grant, *The Bible as Literature,* pp. 13, 14.
[26] See I Samuel 16:1–13.

A revolution, in 842 B.C., put Jehu on the throne. With his dynasty came the decline of the Northern Kingdom. Temporary prosperity was restored with the long reign of Jereboam II. With his death, however, his son, Zachariah, became king but was slain in six months. Subsequently the Northern Kingdom declined so rapidly that the fall of the capital, Samaria, came in 722 B.C., and Israel was carried into captivity.

Religious growth in Judah took a different course from the religious growth in Israel, for in Judah, the Southern Kingdom, the center of unity was the Temple and the priesthood.

> For I will defend this city, to save it, for mine own sake, and for my servant David's sake.
>
> And it came to pass that night, that the angel of the Lord went out, and smote in the camp of the Assyrians an hundred fourscore and five thousand: and when they arose early in the morning, behold, they were all dead corpses. So Sennacherib king of Assyria departed, and went and returned, and dwelt at Ninevah.[27]

Judah remained a vassal of Assyria until about 650 B.C. In 606 B.C. Ninevah fell. Judah became a vassal of the Babylonian empire and attempted to cast off the Babylonian yoke, but in 597 B.C. the king of Babylonia captured Jerusalem:

> And Jehoiachin the king of Judah went out to the king of Babylon, he, and his mother, and his servants, and his princes, and his officers: and the king of Babylon took him in the eighth year of his reign. And he carried out thence all the treasures of the house of the Lord, and the treasures of the king's house, and cut in pieces all the vessels of gold which Solomon king of Israel had made in the temple of the Lord, as the Lord had said. And he carried away all Jerusalem, and all the princes, and all the mighty men of valour, even ten thousand captives, and all the craftsmen and smiths: none remained, save the poorest sort of the people of the

---

[27] II Kings 19:34–36.

land. . . . And all the men of might, even seven thousand, and craftsmen and smiths a thousand, all that
were strong and apt for war, even them the king of
Babylon brought captive to Babylon.[28]

The surrender of the city of Jerusalem resulted in the deportation of the important people of the state in 597 B.C. to Babylon,
including the king, Jehoiachin.

Zedekiah, son of Josiah, and the last king of Judah,[29] was
appointed king by Nebuchadnezzar after the capture of Jerusalem in 597 B.C. He began an intrigue with Moab, Edom, Ammon,
Tyre and Sidon. In 588 B.C. the Babylonian army laid siege to
Jerusalem, Zedekiah was captured, blinded and carried in chains
to Babylon, where Jehoiachin was already a captive. Also his
sons were killed.

There was much suffering during the deportation. Nebuchadnezzar had economic as well as political views. One of his
undertakings was to restore the city of Babylon, and Jews were
used for this restoration. Jews were also used to fill up the
vacant lands resulting from the migration of peasants into cities.
Naturally, too, the population had suffered from wars. Nebuchadnezzar's idea was to make the Jews Babylonian citizens and
to give them grants of land. However, any Jew who was considered dangerous was imprisoned; the Jewish aristocracy was
repressed.

JEREMIAH

Jeremiah's letter to the captives in Babylon was not advice
given to slaves but to people whom he advised to settle down
even in their captivity and plant vineyards. The neighbors of
Palestine settled together in Babylonia, and there was very
little attempt on the part of the Babylonians to change the form
of national life. Though the exiles had great freedom, there was
a sense of depression, perhaps because everyone was compelled

---

[28] II Kings 24:12–14,16.
[29] See II Kings 24:17; II Chronicles 36:10.

to do work for the government, and for noncompliance with this order a penalty of death was inflicted.

There is an interval between the death of Jeremiah and the age in which his prophecies were edited. We find that Jeremiah 39:1–13 is condensed from II Kings 25:1–12 and that Jeremiah 52 is derived from II Kings 24:18 and II Kings 25:27–30.[30] Critics tell us that the Septuagint version points to the fact that Jeremiah's prophecies were once current in smaller collections of prophecies.

EZEKIEL

The Babylonian religion had become attractive to the Jews in exile. In Ezekiel, the eighteenth chapter, there is an attempt to give ethical instructions for Israel in Babylonian captivity. The question arose whether Jahweh could be worshipped in an unclean land. There was some practice of the cult, but it was unofficial. In its place, in order to preserve the religion of the people, there developed a new meaning in the Sabbath.

It is clear from Ezekiel that the thing which the Jews set themselves to do was to teach the people the history of Israel. The Jews taught that God's chosen people had sinned; hence, they were in exile. Up to this time the history of the Jews had not taught this fact. Consequently history had to be rewritten to bring out this fact, and the form that this new idea took was the standard of Deuteronomy. These editors say that there shall be only one place of sacrifice; that is Jerusalem. The Deuteronomic school had taken the standard of one sanctuary, and had taken it as if it had been the law of God from the time of Solomon on. The Priestly school was interested in law; but the Deuteronomic school had been interested in history. Hence, the effort to revise the history began at this time, but the revision did not end with the Exile. The Deuteronomic editors had been interested not in history for its own sake but in history that would teach that the knowledge of God was a gradual growth.

---

[30] See H. E. Ryle, *The Canon of the Old Testament*, p. 115.

The Deuteronomic book itself was found in the Temple by
Hilkiah, the chief priest, in 621 B.C., and the new law book was
placed in the hand of King Josiah. Josiah at once began to
institute a reformation of the cult in accordance with the demands of the Deuteronomic law, and this code became the
fundamental law of the state. The Temple at Jerusalem was
cleansed of foreign worship; all sanctuaries outside of Jerusalem
were destroyed; idolatry was obliterated, and the Passover was
celebrated in Jerusalem.[31]

Up to the time of the fall of Jerusalem, Ezekiel had been
preaching the judgment of God, and after that date he began
teaching reconstruction. There has been much editing of the
book of Ezekiel. However, the book fits in with the attempt to
teach the people in the new way, by means of history.

In pre-exilic times, evil as well as good had to be traced
back to Jahweh; the postexilic religion was more rational than
the pre-exilic because of the influence of foreign religion. Still
another great advance came in the doctrine of the Spirit. In the
ancient times the Spirit of God was regarded as a physical and
intellectual force. The Spirit of Jahweh is on Samson and Saul
for a while, and then withdraws, and they resume their ordinary
life. But in Ezekiel the spirit of God is a moral force that enters
into the life of the people.

AMOS

Let us turn from the Major to one of the Minor Prophets,
Amos, a contemporary of Jeroboam II, who reigned from 783
to 743 B.C. He is consequently generally placed in the period
between 765 and 750 B.C. During Jeroboam's reign, Israel enjoyed a prosperity that had not been equaled since the reign of
Solomon. This prosperity produced materialistic, ease-loving,
self-indulgent people. The belief that had permeated the nation
up to this time was that prosperity was the indisputable evidence of the favor of Jehovah toward Israel, and the Israelites
rejoiced in the confidence that God was with them. They

---

[31] II Kings 22 f.

laughed at Amos and his prophecy that a day of judgment was upon the nation.

Amos had preached nothing but destruction. After the Exile some editor attached to the end of the book the material from chapter 9, verse 11, to the end of the book. Hence in this way the prophecy of destruction and the prophecy of hope were brought together by the editors.

When Amos appeared at Bethel, he condemned the corruption, the injustice, the immorality of the nation. He was convinced that Israel's wickedness would bring inevitable doom and would destroy the nation. This sort of prophecy was not popular at the time it was uttered, and Amos was banished from the Northern Kingdom, but his prophecies were preserved. Amos very likely wrote down himself the visions in the latter part of the book. But what we have of his actual, vigorous utterances was probably written down by editors.

> The Book of Amos has suffered little at the hands of editors. The following passages . . . are regarded as of later origin than the days of Amos. They reflect the historical conditions and the opinions of later times, viz., 1:2, The Theme of the Book; 1:9–10, The Oracle Against Tyre; 1:11–12, Oracle Against Edom; 2:4–5, Oracle Against Judah; 4:12–13 and 5:8–9 and 9:5–6, Doxologies, setting forth the power of God; 6:9–10, detailed expansion of the description of the disease-smitten community; 9:8–15, a modification of the foregoing judgment and a promise for the days to come. . . . Amos came to the front, apparently, with his message clearly formulated in his own mind and found no need to change it afterwards to any serious extent.[32]

HOSEA

The conditions reflected in Hosea's sermons accord well with what is known of the period from 745 to 735 B.C. The pros-

---

[32] John Merlin Powis Smith, *The Books of Amos, Hosea and Micah* (the Macmillan Co., 1914), pp. 2, 3; by permission of the publisher.

perity that had characterized the reign of Jeroboam II rapidly
disappeared upon his death. Internal strife, coupled with foreign
invasion and heavy tribute, made business conditions unstable.
There were murders and conspiracies. There were overtures
made by the government both to Assyria and to Egypt for help.
Hosea realized clearly the weakness and the probable downfall
of his country at the hands of either Assyria or Egypt.

Hosea was a native of the Northern Kingdom, concerned
with the rights of a loving God. Amos had been concerned with
the rights of man. Hosea is dominated by the thought of God's
love for Israel, and is amazed because that love receives no
recognition in Israel.

> The text of the Book of Hosea is one of the worst pre-
> served in the Old Testament. Many passages have been
> so mutilated as to be now unintelligible. Some of these
> can be restored with a fair degree of certainty by the
> aid of the translations into Greek and Syriac, especially
> the Septuagint.[33]

ISAIAH

While Hosea was prophesying in the Northern Kingdom,
Isaiah of Jerusalem was prophesying in the Southern Kingdom
(Judah). While Isaiah was in the Temple in the year 738 B.C.,
he received a vision of his and his people's sinfulness. He was
given, by Yahweh, a commission to speak to his sinful people
and was told that their destruction was to be complete.

> He came to forsee a revolution in Judah too, for here
> also social conditions were unbearable; the king was a
> child and a tool in the hands of women. The revolu-
> tion was to be the judgment of Yahweh. The injustice
> and grinding oppression of the people by the leaders
> and princes, and the haughty, coquettish wantonness of

---

[33] Smith, *op. cit.*, p. 73.

the Jerusalem women, were the reason why he must intervene.[34]

In the book of Isaiah the Sabbath is stressed in the exilic writings as the mark of the Jews. It is a mark to preserve their own peculiar religion. Hence, the Sabbath takes on a new importance.

> For thus saith the Lord unto the eunuchs that keep my sabbaths, and choose the things that please me, and take hold of my covenant; Even unto them will I give in mine house and within my walls a place and a name better than of sons and of daughters: I will give them an everlasting name, that shall not be cut off. Also the sons of the stranger, that join themselves to the Lord, to serve him, and to love the name of the Lord, to be his servants, every one that keepeth the sabbath from polluting it, and taketh hold of my covenant; even them will I bring to my holy mountain, and make them joyful in my house of prayer: their burnt offerings and their sacrifices shall be accepted upon mine altar; for mine house of prayer shall be called an house of prayer for all people.[35]

At this time of the Exile the old laws and customs and cult practices were set down in a code, and were gathered together and made simple by the priesthood. Now, this was the work of the Deuteronomic editors, to show that the knowledge of God had been a gradual growth. They must show that on Sabbath and feast days the old form of worship was used, minus the sacrifice.

The book of Isaiah contains many passages which are not his. The whole second part, from chapter 40 to chapter 66, is merely affixed to Isaiah and was added at the time when the

---

[34] J. A. Bewer, *The Literature of the Old Testament in Its Historical Development*, p. 102.

[35] Isaiah 56:4–7.

prophetical writings were being collected. From chapter 13 to chapter 20 (the oracles against foreign nations), from chapter 24 to chapter 27 (the apocalypse), and from chapter 36 to chapter 39 (the biographical material) we have material not written by Isaiah. Hence we see that the largest part of the collection of oracles in this book is not Isaiah's.

The first part of Isaiah is clearly the work of compilation, to which have been appended both an extract from the Book of Kings[36] and a song of Hezekiah, obtained from some independent collection of national psalms.

Isaiah shows through his prediction of disaster that within five years the nation will be destroyed. Since this prophecy was not fulfilled, he wrote another memoir to justify himself. He says that he may have been mistaken as to the time but he knows that God is going to strike, and that the policy which Ahaz followed can end only in destruction. Chapters 6 to 8 and parts of chapter 9 are the kernel of Isaiah's writings. Another memoir written some time later is that of chapters 28 to 30, in regard to the crisis with Egypt. Other oracles were written by people who heard Isaiah. The chief note in all of Isaiah's utterances was that the nation was going to be destroyed, but that the remnant would survive.

Amos' predictions were fulfilled, but Isaiah's were not fulfilled for more than a hundred years. The fundamental thing to Isaiah was God's character, God's righteousness, God's will; the secondary thing was the fulfilment of Isaiah's prophecies. In Judah a group of people had put Isaiah on a pinnacle, and they were puzzled by the seeming failure of his predictions. He must refer, they thought, not only to Judah but also to Israel and Damascus. The editors, therefore, put in Isaiah: ". . . the land whose two kings thou abhorrest shall be forsaken."[37]

From 700 to 600 B.C. the Kingdom of Judah was the vassal of Assyria. With the deliverance of Jerusalem came the beginning of a growth in the belief that Jerusalem could not be taken. Knowing that Isaiah was in Jerusalem at that time, people fifty

---

[36] II Kings 18–19.
[37] Isaiah 7:16 (R.V.)

years later said that he must have had something to do with
the deliverance of the city.

> And the multitude of all the nations that fight against
> Ariel, even all that fight against her and her munition,
> and that distress her, shall be a dream of night vision.
> It shall even be as when an hungry man dreameth,
> and, behold, he eateth; but he awaketh, and his soul
> is empty: or as when a thirsty man dreameth, and,
> behold, he drinketh; but he awaketh, and, behold, he is
> faint, and his soul hath appetite: so shall the multitude
> of all the nations be, that fight against mount Zion.[38]

The leaders of the Exile carried with them the sacred writings. They read these statements and realized that, more than
one hundred years before, Isaiah had made this prophecy. They
felt that if his prophecies were true, then his doctrine would be
true; hence, the leaders of the Babylonian Exile worked over
and brought up to date not only the prophecies of Isaiah and
the rest of the Latter Prophets but also the Former Prophets
(the prophetic histories). We have shown this work of compilation and redaction in this chapter.

In the second division of the Bible (the Prophets), there
were two kinds of writing. First, the oracle of the prophets had
to do with the prophets' own times and dealt with what they
believed to be the will of God. The second kind of writing com-
prises the oracles edited by a later generation of men who
wanted to bring out clearly what the prophets meant and to try
to make it applicable to all times. Hence the editors are as
important as the prophets themselves.

If a process of special collection was begun in the time of
Nehemiah, that of their selection as sacred Scripture can hardly
have begun until a century later. The Septuagint (or the Greek
translation) of the Prophets was completed before the canonical
character had been determined or recognized in Alexandria.
Critics feel that it was the spread of Hellenic culture which
followed Alexander's victories which contributed to the desire

---

[38] Isaiah 29:7–8.

of the Jewish community to expand their sacred literature—to admit the Prophets for the purpose of public reading in the synagogue.

> The canon of the prophets, comprising the so-called "Former Prophets," i.e., the Books of Joshua, Judges, Samuel, and Kings; and the "Latter Prophets," i.e., Isaiah, Jeremiah, Ezekiel, and the Twelve, was fixed by 200 B.C., but its authority never was as great as that of the law. True enough, the prophets had been God's spokesmen too, and this gave to their words divine sanction. But they were regarded, especially after the formation of the canon of the law, as mere expounders of the law, and as such not in the same class with Moses (cf. Num. 12:6 f.), in spite of their divine inspiration. Indeed, the Book of Ezekiel had difficulty in gaining admission to the canon because it contained some statements which could only with difficulty be harmonized with the law.[39]

---

[39] Bewer, *op. cit.*, pp. 427, 428.

• III •

The Writings

The Writings comprise the third section of the Old Testament canon and mark the third period in its growth. That the ancient Hebrews came to appreciate the need of preserving a large variety of the newer and more miscellaneous books satisfactorily explains the gradual and almost imperceptible formation of the third section of the Old Testament into a definite group called Writings. It took a long time for these books of the third section to win for themselves recognition as Scripture. Ultimately, about the year 100 B.C., the following thirteen books emerged as the third section of the Bible or the canon of the Writings: Psalms, Proverbs, Job, the Song of Songs, Ruth, Lamentations, Ecclesiastes, Esther, Daniel, Ezra, Nehemiah, and I and II Chronicles.

During the interval between the conclusion of the second canon (the Prophets) and the commencement of the third canon (the Writings), men like Jason and Alcimus had brought the high-priesthood to the lowest stage of degradation. Their corruption was followed by the persecution of Antiochus Epiphanes. Religious freedom, however, won; civil liberty was finally obtained, and the old borders were restored.

Jonathan and Simon, brothers of Judas Maccabeus, entered upon a career of national greatness, united by ties of devotion to the religion of Jehovah. This religious revival originated the movement which sought to expand the canon of Hebrew scriptures by the addition of a third group, the Writings.[1]

Antiochus had demanded that copies of the Law be destroyed. This order naturally enhanced the value of the treasure, and preservation of the sacred books was ensured.

PSALMS

In raising to canonicity the Writings, first there had to be made a selection of those writings which had exerted the greatest influence over the spirit of the Jews before and after the Exile. The most important book of the Writings (Kethubim) to obtain admission to the rank of Scripture was the Psalter. The Psalms had been used as the hymnbook of the second Temple, but when the Book of Psalms was raised to canonicity, it became the hymnbook of Israel. In I Chronicles 16:8–36 we find that the chronicler makes free extracts from Psalm 105.

The English Revised Version keeps the division of the Hebrew Psalter into five books: 1–41; 42–72; 73–89; 90–106; 107–150. Each book ends with a doxology, now numbered among the verses of the last Psalm of the book; except the final psalm of the fifth book, all of which is a doxology. This division is old, dating from before the LXX translation, but it is artificial. The Jewish rabbis were probably correct in holding that it was made in imitation of the five books of the Pentateuch. The real division is into three groups: (1) 1–41, (2) 42–89, (3) 90–150. (1) uses Jehovah mostly for the divine name; (2) uses Elohim mostly; (3) uses Jehovah exclusively, except in 108 and 144–149. Psalms are repeated in the different groups, sometimes with

---

[1] H. E. Ryle, *The Canon of the Old Testament*, p. 134.

the divine name changed. Compare 14 and 53; 40, 13–17 and 71. It is evident that the present book of Psalms was made up of three books, which contained different editions of a few hymns, and which used by preference different names for God. Then, before the triple division had been forgotten, some editor divided two of the three books, naming five divisions.[2]

Those which are usually assigned to the opening of the Exile, as songs which present the memory of the captives' journey from Palestine to Babylon, are Psalms 42 and 43. Some critics, however, connect these Psalms with earlier captivities of parts of northern Israel. Psalms 89, 120, 121, and 122 may be exilic psalms which show both a sense of suffering and a confidence that God will give his blessing to the nation.

The whole range of human life, its joys and its woe, its light and its shadow, and its daily routine, is treated in the Psalter. There are psalms of common worship, pilgrim songs and processional hymns, calls to worship, hymns of praise and thanksgiving for individual or national deliverance, for the harvest and the joys of nature. There are national psalms, prayers for deliverance from external or internal foes, for national restoration, prayers of trust in national peril and of praise for past deliverance, battle songs and odes of victory. There are royal psalms, coronation and wedding odes, prayers for the king's just and ideal rule, for God's help in battle or thanksgiving for victory. There are psalms of individual piety with its longings for communion with God and its joy in the experience of it; with its prayers for help and healing, for forgiveness and purification; with its songs of faith and trust and its hymns of thanksgiving and praise. There are didactic psalms, with the warm, insistent teaching of the fear of God, the divine government in the world, retribution for

---

[2] Wood and Grant, *The Bible as Literature*, p. 164.

pious and wicked alike; with their warnings against
trust in riches, and concerning the vanity and brevity
of life; with their teachings of true worship and true
sacrifice, of the blessedness of forgiveness and of chari-
tableness toward others, of the joys of home and of
nature and law; and with their lessons from Israel's
great history in the past. . . . They are not grouped
according to any chronological, topical or other principle. Varied as life itself, they are also tossed together
in the same kaleidoscopic manner as life's experiences
themselves.[3]

Some of the Psalms are perhaps as old as David, but the
collections in our Psalter date from the period of the second
Temple. After the Temple was rebuilt, the old forms and rituals
were adhered to, although modifications were made, and the
old and new hymns were called "the Psalms of David." However, in the final edition of the Psalter we have the five books of
praises, corresponding to the five books of the Law.

Seventy-three of the one hundred and fifty psalms are
directly assigned to David. Many of the rest are ascribed to
various other great Hebrew worthies, among them Moses, the
sons of Korah, and Solomon. But the trend of critics today is to
reduce the emphasis upon Davidic Psalms and to teach that
the value of a Psalm depends upon the Psalm itself and not
upon the author. The date of Psalms, naturally, is uncertain.

"Create in me a clean heart, O God; and renew a right spirit
within me."[4] David, in this plea, reaches the highest spiritual
level, for he laments his sin, not because he is being punished
but because it has offended God. He asks for forgiveness, for
cleansing, for a renewed gift of the spirit of God. This is peni-
tence that is fruit of the prophetic religion.

At the time that the Prophets became canonical, there existed among the Jews an extensive religious literature outside
the limits of the canon. Ecclesiastes (Koheleth) sighs over the
number of books and the weariness of the flesh resulting:

---

[3] J. A. Bewer, *The Literature of the Old Testament in Its Historical
Development*, pp. 340–41.
  [4] Psalm 51:10.

The words of the wise are as goads, and as nails
fastened by the masters of assemblies, which are given
from one shepherd. And further, by these, my son, be
admonished: of making many books there is no end;
and much study is a weariness of the flesh.[5]

This statement was made by Ecclesiastes in the third century
B.C. We therefore ask ourselves why books like Ezra, Nehemiah,
Ruth, Esther, and I and II Chronicles were not included among
the narrative books of the Prophets. We further ask why Daniel
and Lamentations were not among the prophetical writings.

Critics tell us that Ruth, Ecclesiastes, Lamentations, and
the Song of Songs were excluded because of subject matter.
Ezra, Esther, Nehemiah, and I and II Chronicles were excluded
from the Prophets because of the recency of their composition
and, also, because of their subject matter. Daniel and the
Psalms were excluded because compilations had not yet been
completed when the canon of the Prophets was concluded in
200 B.C.

PROVERBS

"Wisdom literature" is the term used to designate the books
of Proverbs, Job and Ecclesiastes. Proverbs is an example of a
work that has been gradually compiled. There are three or
four stages revealed in the structure of compilation. The an-
tiquity of its contents (fourth century B.C.), the name of Solomon associated with the authorship of the early part, and its
moral strength, all of these factors tend to place Proverbs in the
highest repute. Proverbs deals with national events and national religion. It is the simplest expression of Hebrew wisdom.

It is a miscellaneous collection of eight pamphlets and
a preface, presenting different literary forms and coming from different authors in different times. The unity
lies in the purpose and in the general type of literature. The purpose is expressed in the preface (Proverbs
1:1–6) as being instruction in morals and good living.[6]

---

[5] Ecclesiastes 12:11–12.
[6] Wood and Grant, *op. cit.*, p. 172.

In Proverbs, chapter 1 to 9, there is a long discussion on wisdom and wise conduct. The fundamental principle is stated: "The fear of the Lord is the beginning of knowledge; but fools despise wisdom and instruction."[7] This idea of the recognition of God's power was stated by Isaiah: "The lofty looks of men shall be humbled, and the haughtiness of men shall be bowed down, and the Lord alone shall be exalted in that day."[8]

These two ideas expressed in the Writings and in the Prophets are different from the idea expressed in the Law:

> And all the people saw the thunderings, and the lightnings, and the noise of the trumpet, and the mountain smoking: and when the people saw it, they removed, and stood afar off.[9]

In Proverbs 8 wisdom is represented as the controller of life and the attendant of Jahweh at creation. From this chapter (which is the beginning of Part II) to the conclusion of the book, the material is quite different from the material in the first seven chapters. Tradition ascribes the authorship of Part I to Solomon. But the core of the book is from chapter 10 through chapter 29. This material is a collection of aphorisms or proverbs in couplet form. There is no nationalism expressed in Proverbs, nor were the editors interested in cult; but honesty, truthfulness, justice, kindness, political equity, family life, and the virtue of love are stressed. Again and again the idea is reiterated that goodness is rewarded by prosperitiy and sin by distress.

JOB

Proverbs seems to be a preface to Job, for suffering is one of the problems of the Old Testament. Before the Exile the nation was treated as a unit, as God's chosen people. But during the Exile the individual came into prominence, and there immediately arose the problems of the individual and of suffer-

---

[7] Proverbs 1:7.
[8] Isaiah 2:11.
[9] Exodus 20:18.

ing. Job, then, in contrast to Proverbs, deals with a personal experience and speculative questions.

> Job becomes a self-determined epic of the soul, march-
> ing by its own laws to its own dramatic crises and
> reaching its serene finale in a spirit far more akin to
> that of Dante's *Comedy* than to that of the original
> poem.[10]

The theology of the Book of Job is an advanced theology. Some critics feel that Job is an attempt to carry out the idea of the individual just as the idea of the nation has been carried out. Other critics feel that, except for the epilogue, the Book of Job is a condemnation of God by a school of skeptics who believed that the problem of suffering could not be solved, that God did not care if man suffered.

The prologue asks, "Why do the righteous suffer?" and answers, "To satisfy Satan." Job's comforters answer this question in terms of Old Testament theology (with the exception of Proverbs, the Prophets and the poetical books), "Do good and you will prosper." Eliphaz says: "Behold, happy is the man whom God correcteth: therefore despise not thou the chastening of the Almighty."[11] Elihu talks to Job in terms of Old Testament theology:

> For the work of man shall he render unto him, and
> cause every man to find according to his ways. Yea,
> surely God will not do wickedly, neither will the Al-
> mighty pervert judgment.[12]

One of the editors of Job tells us that the real reason for Job's suffering is that he is being tried, that God gave and God has taken away.

The book of Job is made up of a prose introduction, the prologue; a poem, an epical drama on a magnificent scale (but the dialogue of the drama is given undramatically); and a prose

---

[10] J. H. Wicksteed, *A Study of Blake's Vision of the Book of Job,* p. 13.
[11] Job 5:17.
[12] Job 34:11–12.

conclusion. The epilogue is written in an entirely different style from the rest of the book, showing that the man who wrote the poem could not have written the epilogue.

In the prologue, Job retains his integrity, but when we turn to the poetry,[13] we find an entirely different Job who curses his day. Job wants to find a God who will square with his ideas of justice, for he feels that he is suffering unjustly. One of the later editors evidently felt the need of saving Job's orthodoxy; hence we have the epilogue, the happy ending. What the final editor did, however, was to point out magnificently that there were factors about which men know nothing, that there are regions of truth that the mind has not discovered.

One of the most remarkable passages on immortality in the Old Testament is "though . . . worms destroy this body, yet in my flesh shall I see God."[14]

The date of the book of Job is post-exilic, about 300 B.C.

> The origin of the story cannot be traced. . . . There are elements of folklore in the repetition, the systematic development, and the simple directness of the prologue and epilogue. The long and elaborate speeches, on the other hand, are not folktale, but literary development. The author has adapted this old story to his own purpose. It is as futile to ask how much he has changed it as it would be to ask that question of Tennyson's *Idyls of the King,* were all our knowledge of the legend of King Arthur derived from these poems.[15]

ECCLESIASTES

Ecclesiastes (Koheleth, or the Preacher) originated almost at the end of the religious development, about the year 200 B.C. It was written by a man who belonged to the same circle as the authors of the book of Job. Tradition ascribes this book to Solomon, but scholarship denies this. The designation Ecclesi-

---

13 Job 3–31.
14 Job 19:26 (The R.V., though somewhat different, is still remarkable).
15 Wood and Grant, *op. cit.,* pp. 190–91.

astes taken in the sense of one who addresses an ecclesia (an assembly) is an attempt on the part of the Greek translator of the book to render the Hebrew word *Koheleth* (Preacher), which is the name assumed by the author of the book.

> Koheleth lived at a time when the author had begun to be a factor in the intellectual and social life, but still could hide himself under a nom de plume and reap an advantage from so doing. For Koheleth is a disguise, and it is reasonable to suppose that in describing himself as a king over Jerusalem who had amassed wealth, who possessed great power, and who was also "wiser than all who were before me in Jerusalem" (1:16) he aimed to identify himself with Solomon, whose name must, therefore, have already become at the time Koheleth wrote a synonym for wisdom, glory and power. The device was successful. An uncritical tradition, accepting the implication in the disguise, attributed the book to Solomon. The magic of this name went a long way towards overcoming the objections that later arose against its inclusion in the canon because of its heterodox spirit and contents.[16]

Ecclesiastes is a series of charming and witty informal essays the unity of which consists in their common disillusionment. We should picture the author as a man who smiles at the vanity of the things he once coveted. He has no system of philosophy and is a free lance in religion. His interest in Judaism is merely his interest in the religion around him. He seems to think that neither work nor play is the aim of life, that there is no aim.

> And I gave my heart to know wisdom, and to know madness and folly: I perceived that this also is vexation of spirit.[17]

Koheleth (Ecclesiastes) goes one step further than Job. Job attacked the orthodox view that suffering was the result of

---

[16] Morris Jastrow, Jr., *A Gentle Cynic*, pp. 65–66.
[17] Ecclesiastes 1:17.

sin. Koheleth tells us that there is no purpose to life. Life is given to us to be enjoyed or wasted, and the best thing one can do is to smile at the sorrows of life.

The doctrine of the prophets has been that God was working out his purpose in the history of his people. Ecclesiastes, however, says that this world is a place where man may get his reward or he may not. He feels that the only purpose in life is to keep busy with the duties of life and to laugh at the ills of life.

In Jerusalem at this time were two parties, the Sadducees (the priesthood, who were worldly and politically minded) and those who were later to develop into the party of Pharisees (the pious, conventional, rigid, exclusive nationalistic group). Between these were the skeptics, men who felt that the cult was merely a foolish survival. To this group belong the authors of the main part of Job and of Ecclesiastes. These men were gentle cynics. They did not wish to be taken too seriously, for they spoke ironically rather than bitterly.

Ecclesiastes furnishes evidence that there was a non-legalistic school who scorned the Priestly code and the chroniclers. This non-legalistic orthodoxy we find expressed in Proverbs, Job, and Ecclesiastes. Though legalism eventually became orthodox, it took such authors as those of Job and Ecclesiastes to make it such.

The conclusion of Ecclesiastes is: "Fear God, and keep his commandments: for this is the whole duty of man."[18] This seems to have been added by an editor in the interests of orthodoxy, for it is not consonant with the rest of the book.

The inclusion of the Book of Ecclesiastes in the Canon of the Writings was one of the old disputes between the rival schools of Shammai and Hillel, the former rejecting, the latter accepting the book as sacred; and the decision at Jamnia did not secure unanimity of opinion. Not only does a contemporary of the Patriarch Judah assert that while the Song of Songs is canonical because it

---

[18] Ecclesiastes 12:13.

was spoken by the holy spirit, Ecclesiastes is not, because it is Solomon's own wisdom, but Jerome, at the end of the fourth century, heard from his Jewish teachers that it had been proposed to commit the book to oblivion on internal grounds, but the rabbis had been withheld from doing so by the closing words (Ecclesiastes 12, 13 f.), which of themselves warranted putting it among the divine books.[19]

Akiba said about the Song of Songs:

God forbid! No man in Israel ever dissented about the Song of Songs, holding it not to be sacred. The whole age altogether is not worth as much as the day on which the Song of Songs was given to Israel; for all the Scriptures are holy, but the Song of Songs is the holiest of all. If there was a division, it was only over Ecclesiastes.[20]

THE SONG OF SONGS

In the Song of Songs, we have one of the most perfect specimens of early Hebrew poetry. It is derived from the best period of Hebrew literature. The theme is secular, and allusions to the book are not found in literature before the Christian era. The book was interpreted by the two rival schools of Shammai and Hillel as being of Solomonic authorship and as being an allegory of the love of God and the Jewish people.

The Song of Songs is a standing drama of thought rather than of action and may be compared with Browning's and Landor's works. It was admitted to the canon of Writings at Jamnia in A.D. 90, because the rabbis felt that the Holy Spirit rested upon Solomon and that he spoke three books—Proverbs, Ecclesiastes, and the Song of Songs.

---

[19] Reprinted by permission of the publishers from George Foot Moore's *Judaism in the First Centuries of the Christian Era* (Cambridge, Mass.: Harvard University Press, 1927), Vol. I, pp. 242–43.

[20] *Ibid.*, p. 243.

I am black, but comely, O ye daughters of Jerusalem,
As the tents of Kedar, as the curtains of Solomon.[21]

Solomon had a vineyard at Baal-hamon;
He let out the vineyard unto keepers;
Every one of the fruit thereof was to bring a thousand
    pieces of silver.
My vineyard, which is mine, is before me:
Thou, O Solomon, must have a thousand,
And those that keep the fruit thereof two hundred.[22]

"Solomon" is an insertion into the text; it breaks into the metre. The Song of Songs was in existence at about 300 B.C.

LAMENTATIONS

Lamentations was supposed to record the elegy of Jeremiah over the destruction of Jerusalem. In the Septuagint, Lamentations followed Jeremiah, and the Greek translation prefaces the book as follows:

And it came to pass, after Israel was led into captivity
and Jerusalem laid waste, that Jeremiah sat weeping,
and lamented with this lamentation over Jerusalem.[23]

Chapters 2 and 4 evidently came from the Jews of royal circles who had been repressed in Babylon by Nebuchadnezzar. Chapter 2 is given over largely to the description of God's anger to his people. The agony of the people, the famine within the city, and the contempt that other nations feel for them in their disaster are described.

The terrible scenes of the famine, the pitiful cry of the
babies for food and drink, the ghostly sight of faces
black and withered from suffering, and the horror of

---

[21] Song of Songs 1:5.
[22] Song of Songs 8:11–12.
[23] See Bewer, *op. cit.*, p. 191.

mothers eating the flesh of their own children were unforgettable.[24]

Critics agree that Lamentations consists of five independent anonymous poems, all dealing with the calamities that befell Judah and Jerusalem because of the siege and capture of the city by the Chaldeans in 586 B.C.

Chapter 2 does not sound as if it were written by the author of chapter 1, which is similar to Jeremiah's belief that the Chaldeans were chosen by God to chasten his people.

> The yoke of my transgressions is bound by his hand: they are wreathed, and come up upon my neck: he hath made my strength to fall, the Lord hath delivered me into their hands, from whom I am not able to rise up.[25]

Jeremiah could not have written:

> Her gates are sunk into the ground; he hath destroyed and broken her bars: her king and her princes are among the Gentiles: the law is no more; her prophets also find no vision from the Lord.[26]

It was quite natural that these poems should have been ascribed to Jeremiah, for he was the only inspired author of that period whose name was handed down to posterity. The names of the real authors are unknown.

I AND II CHRONICLES

In the Prophets we found that the first history of the Jewish monarchy was given in the books of Judges, I Samuel, II Samuel, I Kings, and II Kings. This history ended with the destruction of Jerusalem by Nebuchadnezzar, the king of Babylon, in 586 B.C. This first history is dated about 600 B.C.

---

[24] *Ibid.*, p. 189.
[25] Lamentations 1:14.
[26] Lamentations 2:9.

In the Writings the second history, or the history of the Kingdom of Judah from the accession of Saul to the rebuilding of Jerusalem, is written in I Chronicles, II Chronicles, Ezra and Nehemiah. This second history is dated from about 300 B.C. and includes the restoration of Jerusalem under Artaxerxes, the king of Persia.

I and II Chronicles are a product of a group of men who took it upon themselves to rewrite history in the light of representatives of the Priestly code. The writing of Chronicles is the final step in the history of Israel being transformed into church history. The chronicler, a priest or a singer in the choir, was interested in David, anointed by God. He refused to besmirch the character of David by repeating the unfavorable stories about him found in Samuel. This second history included neither David's adultery with Bath-sheba and his murder of Uriah, her husband, nor the rebellion of Absalom. David appears in Chronicles as a king without defeat and without reproach. There is mention neither of war with Saul, by which he seized the throne, nor of conspiracy of his son Adonijah to take the throne away from him in his old age. This picture of David is one of the few exceptions in the Bible of a character dealt with romantically rather than realistically.

Chronicles does not report Solomon's folly. Both the first and the second history agree as to Solomon's reign of splendor, his prosperity and his wisdom. The second history, however, magnifies Solomon as a builder of the Temple and many cities, and the children of Israel are not made his servants but his men of war.

In the first history we are told that the burden of compulsory service was on the children of Israel. This service was so severe that when Solomon died the children of Israel demanded better treatment from Rehoboam.

Another omission in the second history is that of the annals of the Northern Kingdom. The writers of both the first and the second histories belonged to the tribe of Judah. But when the schism came and the two kingdoms were divided, the northern tribes were led by Ephraim and the southern by Judah; the

Northern Kingdom set up shrines and came no more to the
Temple at Jerusalem. The writer of the second history says that
this was an act so hateful to God that the Northern Kingdom
should henceforth be cast out of remembrance. Hence the
Northern Kingdom was given no space in the chronicler's
record.[27]

There are two series of histories of Israel in the Old
Testament. One is the series of books from Genesis to
Kings; the other the books of Chronicles, Ezra and
Nehemiah. The first series is composed of at least
three separate works—the Hexateuch, Judges, and Sam-
uel-Kings. The second was originally a single book,
from one author. Both begin with Adam, but the second
series covers the time before the kingdom merely by
genealogies, omitting all the stories which made the
early books of the other series such excellent literature.
The real history begins with David. The books of
Chronicles duplicate II Samuel and Kings; Ezra and
Nehemiah contain postexilic history not covered in the
first series.[28]

The first series of histories, which we called "prophetic"
through the source P, appears in the first six books of the Old
Testament. The second history is interested in the ritual worship
of the Temple, the relation of sin and suffering, of prosperity
and goodness, and in God's guidance of Israel.

For his sources, the chronicler had Samuel and Kings, a Book
of Kings of Judah and Israel (also an expansion of these books),
a collection of early prophets Nathan, Gad, Iddo and others,
and the book of Isaiah. The chronicler does not tell a story as
the writers of the first histories did but points out his moral in
the most pedantic way:

So Saul died for his transgression which he committed
against the Lord, even against the word of the Lord,

---

[27] See George Hodges, *How to Know the Bible*, pp. 83 ff.
[28] Wood and Grant, *op. cit.*, p. 142.

which he kept not, and also for asking counsel of one
that had a familiar spirit, to enquire of it.[29]

The chronicler was so much interested in the Temple at
Jerusalem, in the priests and Levites (the ministers of Yahweh),
and in the Levitical singers and musicians that one feels he must
have been a singer himself. His interests were primarily ecclesiastical, and he wrote probably in the third century B.C. He began
his story with Adam and ended it with Ezra and Nehemiah. His
unhistorical point of view is due to the chronicler's belief in the
existence of the Priestly Law and of organized hierocracy from
the beginning. The chronicler gives us a pious tale rather than
history.

> The books of Ezra and Nehemiah were originally part
> of the chronicler's work, for his interest in the temple
> led him to write the story of the second temple also,
> beginning with the edict of Cyrus and ending with the
> work of Nehemiah and Ezra, through whom the temple
> was protected and the law introduced and enforced.
> He used here as his sources the Second Isaiah, Haggai,
> and Zechariah, the Aramaic history and the memoirs of
> Ezra and Nehemiah, besides some genealogical lists
> extending to the time of Alexander the Great.[30]

NEHEMIAH

Nehemiah was appointed governor by Artaxerxes I to rebuild
the walls of Jerusalem. Since he had no spiritual authority, he
went back to Babylonia and persuaded Ezra to go to Jerusalem
with a new code of laws to be enforced rigidly. Nehemiah took
certain action in the case of mixed marriages, but this action
was more general than that taken by Ezra. Nehemiah might be
regarded as the secular official, while, at his request, Ezra came
to work out the spiritual reformation.

---

[29] I Chronicles 10:13.
[30] Bewer, *op. cit.*, pp. 301–2.

The chronicler seems not to have liked the idea of the state's coming before the church; hence, he gave Ezra the first place in this history and Nehemiah the second.

Nehemiah, in chapters 3, 4, and 6, tells of the building of the walls of Jerusalem. The high priests were opposed to the principles of Nehemiah, for they were ecclesiastical, and civil leaders and the policy of exclusiveness cut them off from pleasant cultural influences of the outside world. If the priesthood is not entirely spiritual, there will be divided allegiance, and secular advantages will appear greater than spiritual advantages. Nehemiah, however, adroitly turned aside political opposition, and the walls of Jerusalem were finished. He also established decent laws in Jerusalem.

> So the wall was finished in the twenty and fifth day of the month Elul, in fifty and two days.[31]
> And the rulers of the people dwelt at Jerusalem: the rest of the people also cast lots, to bring one of ten to dwell in Jerusalem, the holy city, and nine parts to dwell in other cities. And the people blessed all the men, that willingly offered themselves to dwell at Jerusalem.[32]

The priests and Levites were to live within the walls of Jerusalem, but when these walls were dedicated trouble began. Social conditions were bad because of the shifting of the population. The wealthy, too, were trying to make profits. Nehemiah did the best he could to remedy the situation. He took action to insure decent living conditions for the Levites and also to enforce the Sabbath. Emphasis on the Sabbath was the result of the Exile, because it set the Israelites off from the other people.

In the ninth chapter of Nehemiah, we are told of the merciful dealings of God with His people. This chapter is limited to events included within the range of the Pentateuchal literature. Nehemiah is of great value both as history and literature. This

---

[31] Nehemiah 6:15.
[32] Nehemiah 11:1–2.

memoir is written in the first person by a person who hopes that
God will remember the labors through which he has gone.

> Nehemiah wrote his story after he had returned to the
> royal court of Artaxerxes in 432 B.C. from his governor-
> ship in Jerusalem. In a simple, straightforward, vivid
> manner he told how in the year 445 B.C., when he was
> the king's cupbearer, at the Persian court, he learned
> to his utter dismay of the ruined condition of the walls
> of Jerusalem; how he gained the king's permission to
> rebuild them; how he accomplished the work in an
> incredibly short time in spite of determined opposition
> within and without Jerusalem; how he enlarged the
> population of the city; and how he celebrated the dedi-
> cation of the walls by a solemn festival. Twelve years
> later, in 433 B.C., he came again to Jerusalem and cor-
> rected certain abuses in connection with the temple,
> the payment of the Levites, the observance of the Sab-
> bath, and the intermarriage with foreigners.[33]

EZRA

Ezra was a priest, had studied the Law in Babylonia, and
was filled with the desire to go back to Jerusalem in order to
establish it there. He, with 38 Levites and 220 Nethinim, went
to Jerusalem.

> For I was ashamed to require of the king a band of
> soldiers and horsemen to help us against the enemy in
> the way: because we had spoken to the king, saying,
> The hand of our God is upon all them for good that
> seek him.[34]

The Book of Ezra has suffered at the hands of the editor,
who changed the autobiographical form into the biographical.[35]
The editor was the chronicler, and his point of view is identical

---

[33] Bewer, *op. cit.*, p. 280.
[34] Ezra 8:22.
[35] See Ezra 10 and Nehemiah 8–10.

to Ezra's. For this reason he had been erroneously regarded as the author of these memoirs.

Nehemiah and Ezra won out in their fight against mixed marriages.

> And they made an end with all the men that had taken strange wives by the first day of the first month.[36]

RUTH

But there were men of nobler build, and to one of them we owe the most charming of all love stories, Ruth. This little idyl was, perhaps, included in the Writings because it was the story of mixed marriage, for it showed that David was the product of such a marriage. The author of Ruth is too great an artist to append a lesson. Even though Ruth were a hated Moabite whom the Law would not allow to become a Jew,[37] God blessed her marriage with Boaz, and they became the ancestors of Israel's greatest king.

ESTHER

The Book of Esther was written about 300 B.C. against the Gentiles' hatred for the Jews, against their accusations of unkindness and avarice. The name of God is not mentioned in this book. It was admitted to the canon of the Writings, however, partly because of nationalism and partly because of the feast of Purim.

The Book of Esther may be called an historical novel rather than history, for there are many errors, just as there are in Shakespeare's plays, for the sake of greater effectiveness of the plot. One part of the historical novel has to do with the intercession of Esther with the king to revoke Haman's decree of the Jewish massacre. The Jews massacred 500 men in Susa and Haman's ten sons. In the province, 75,000 people lost their lives at the hands of the Jews, and the Jews celebrated a festival called Purim to commemorate this victory.

---

[36] Ezra 10:17.
[37] Deuteronomy 23:3 and Nehemiah 13:1–3.

When in the third century Johanan said that (in the
days of the Messiah) the books of the Prophets and the
Hagiographa were destined to be abrogated, but the
five books of the Law will not be abrogated, Simon ben
Lakish amended him, saying that the roll of Esther also
and the rules of the traditional law (Halakah) will not
pass away; while an array of rabbis, including Bar
Kuppura and Joshua ben Levi, declared, as has been
noted above, that the roll of Esther was spoken to
Moses from Sinai.[38]

DANIEL

The Book of Daniel, long supposed to be the work of Daniel
who lived in Babylon at the time of the Exile, was written
about 165 B.C. It came from one of the most tragic periods of
Jewish history. Judah from 168 to 164 B.C. was controlled by
Syria, whose king was Antiochus IV. He tried to unify his
empire by putting down the native faiths and substituting the
Greek religion. But Mattathias, an old priest, refused to sacrifice
to the Greek gods, struck down the captain who ordered the
sacrifice, and also the Jew who proposed to offer the sacrifices.
He, with his five sons, then fled to the wilderness of Judah,
where he died the next year. His son, Judas, was a military
genius and won national freedom for the Jews.

From the period which produced the beginning of the
Maccabean war came the book of Daniel. The object
of the book is to encourage the people to hold fast to
their religion in the midst of their persecutions to which
they were subject. When read in the light of its origin
it is one of the most inspiring of the Old Testament
books. Considered apart from its origin, it is a hopeless
tangle of obscure symbolism and historical incongruities.[39]

---

[38] Moore, *op. cit.*, Vol. I, p. 243 (quoted by permission of the Harvard
University Press).

[39] Wood and Grant, *op. cit.*, p. 214.

Biographical sketches of Daniel and his friends are inserted among his prophecies. Chapters 2–7 represent the development of world powers from an historical point of view, while chapters 8–12 represent the development of world powers in relation to Israel. Israel looked forward to the Messianic time for spiritual salvation and for the visible restoration of the kingdom.

Chapter 2 gives one of the simplest visions, and its purpose is to encourage the Jews and to show them that the kingdom which is persecuting them is weak, and that in due time God will overthrow it. Chapter 7 covers the same ground as chapter 2, but with greater emphasis on the suffering of the people and the overthrow of the enemy. Chapter 8 exults in the hope of Antiochus' overthrow by the power of God. There is a reference to the desecration of the Temple, which had stopped the sacrifices.

The Jews had the idea that Jeremiah had said that the Exile was to last only seventy years. The people were allowed to return within seventy years, but since the domination of the foreigners still remained in the year 165 B.C., that prediction became troublesome. In chapter 9 there is an explanation of this period of time, and from this calculation a message for Israel is given, a message to hold firm a few more years and God will bring this period to a close triumphantly. In chapter 12 there is a prediction which is a distinct advance toward the idea of immortality:

> And many of them that sleep in the dust of the earth shall awake, some to everlasting life, and some to shame and everlasting contempt. And they that be wise shall shine as the brightness of the firmament; and they that turn many to righteousness as the stars for ever and ever.[40]

The Book of Daniel was written in Aramaic because it was intended to appeal to the masses, who spoke Aramaic at that time. The opening and closing chapters were translated into Hebrew in order that it might be placed in the canon of the

---

[40] Daniel 12:2–3.

Writings. Since it was purported to have been written in the past to foretell the future, it necessarily had to take the form of a vision.

At the time Daniel was written, the day of the prophets was at an end, for the people believed that prophetic inspiration had ceased. They did not think that this vehicle was a fraud, for most subsequent apocalypses used this same device. The canon of the Prophets had been closed when the Book of Daniel appeared, and in spite of the fact that it was a prophetic book, it could not be included in the second canon. It, therefore, had to be placed in the third canon of the Writings.

CONCLUSION

In choosing the books for the Writings, the final selection was determined by the books which contained the message of God to the Jews which had helped them at all times. In order to be included in the canon, a book must be inspired by God; it must be of ancient date (before 300 B.C.), and it must have some definite connection with David or Solomon. For this reason only the Psalms, Proverbs, Job, the Song of Songs, Ruth, Lamentations, Ecclesiastes, Esther, Daniel, Ezra, Nehemiah, and I and II Chronicles were included in the canon of the Writings. There was much dispute about Esther, the Song of Songs and Ecclesiastes.

At this time, Palestine was overrun with books. No sooner had the Writings been affiliated with the Law and the Prophets than a fourth division, the Apocrypha, began to grow. Someone had to call a halt. The growth of the Old Testament was stopped by an exclusion act, for the rabbis were determined that the Scriptures were to consist of only three sections, the Law, the Prophets, and the Writings.

At the council of Jamnia in A.D. 90 an authoritative list of sacred writings was fixed, and the completed Hebrew Bible emerged, as we have it today. The fight put up by the rabbis against the Gospels, particularly by Akiba and his contemporaries at Jamnia, was filled with enough alarm to bring the Hebrew Bible to a close so that no other writings could be regarded as Sacred Scripture.

PART TWO

The New Testament

· IV ·

The Compilation of the New Testament

The canon of the Old Testament was the model on which the New Testament canon was formed. The Law, the Prophets, and the Writings were the background of the formation of the New Testament. The New Testament was written under the shadow of the Old Testament, for Paul wrote his letters to meet the local needs in preaching the Gospel of Jesus to the Greeks.

Jesus showed an instinctive reverence for the Old Testament, and his relation to the prophetic spirit is close. Jesus' attitude, though, is a discriminating one, combining an acceptance of its statements of spiritual truth with criticism of its moral imperfections. The regard for the Old Testament is shown in Jesus' critical treatment of it and the modified authority which Paul ascribes to it. "All scripture is given by inspiration of God, and is profitable for doctrine, for reproof, for correction, for instruction in righteousness."[1]

The necessity for a second or a Christian part of the Bible was not at first obvious, for the Christians as well as the Jews had their sacred book in the Old Testament. They believed that they understood the Law and the Prophets in a deeper and

[1] II Timothy 3:16.

truer sense than the Jews and, hence, felt that they could regard themselves as its real owners. The Christians, too, believed in the approaching end of the world, and naturally this idea did not direct their thoughts to an enlargement of their Scriptures.

The first step, however, toward a New Testament canon was made when it became the custom, in public worship, to read aloud Christian writings along with the sacred books of the Old Testament. This custom gradually raised these Christian writings to the rank of biblical books. The Gospels, four of which were regarded as canonical in the second half of the second century, were naturally the first Christian writings to attain this rank.[2]

At this time there was an heretical tendency to a Christianity influenced by the great religious movement traveling from the East to the West called Gnosticism. Gnosticism used mythology, mystery, and philosophical speculation and a secret wisdom which made the Gnostic a sharer in the Divine World. References to these ideas are found in the canonical and extra-canonical writings.

Marcion constructed for his Gnostic church a canon in two parts, which was made up of Luke's Gospel and ten Pauline epistles, both of which were purified. The church, in turn, made a similar canon in two parts, which was made up of the four Gospels and some apostolic writings. The Revelation of John was canonized early, although its inclusion in the canon was attacked in the Greek church of the fourth and fifth centuries, in spite of its recognition in the West. Similarly, Acts' relation to the Gospel of Luke helped the inclusion of Acts in the canon. The thirteen Pauline letters, however, were the kernel of the apostolic section. Of those seven epistles with a general address, only I Peter and I John were considered canonical at about A.D. 200. The non-canonical writings, even though they were read aloud in the churches, were gradually lowered in rank, and "Apocrypha" (or "secret writings") was the term used for them. Authorship and contents guided theologians in choosing or

---

[2] See Martin Dibelius, *A Fresh Approach to the New Testament and Early Christian Literature,* pp. 20 ff.

rejecting books to be included in the New Testament. The work of constructing the canon was conditioned by a variety of historical causes. The great purpose for constructing this canon was to plant the message about Christ and yet preserve its peculiar content.

New Testament language is colored by idioms and phrases borrowed from the Old Testament because of the familiarity of these writers with the Old Testament. New Testament language corresponds to the spoken Greek of the first century A.D. rather than to the Greek literary convention. Paul is a master of language, occasionally breaking into poetry. The author of Hebrews follows more nearly the Greek literary convention than any of the New Testament authors. Luke and the author of I Peter write correctly and easily. Mark's Gospel and the book of Revelation are vivid and expressive, yet the language is frequently uncouth. Jesus' sayings may justly be classed among the most exalted passages in all literature.

The books of the Old Testament extend over a period of approximately one thousand years, while the books of the New Testament extend over a period of almost exactly a hundred years. The books of the New Testament were written between A.D. 50 and 150 at various places in the Greek world, and by various hands. Paul's First Epistle to the Thessalonians, written probably in A.D. 51, is agreed to be the earliest of the New Testament books. The Second Epistle of Peter dates about A.D. 150. The larger number of books of the New Testament belong to the sixty years between A.D. 50 and 110.

Palestinian literature is preserved for us as it was incorporated in the Gospels. Mark was probably written in Rome, Matthew in Antioch, while Hebrews and I Peter must also have come from Rome.

In the New Testament, therefore, we have a collection of writings which come to us from many different places, and to this we must attribute not a little of its value. The early churches were not united in a single system as they were in a later age. Each of them stood by itself and developed its own character and its peculiar type of teaching. The New Testament is thus a fully representative book. We have the common gospel put before us in all its various aspects by writers who worked, for the most part, independently of each other.[3]

In the time of Paul, Christianity had broken with Judaism, and toward the end of the first century its converts were mainly from the Gentile world. However, its teachers were men of Jewish origin. Jesus tried to set religion free from the tyranny of the written Law, as it was interpreted by the scribes. He left no written word, but in the expansion of the church, early Christian writings became necessary as a substitute for the living presence of Jesus. When Peter's voice could no longer be heard telling of Jesus' ministry, death and resurrection, the earliest Gospel narrative became a necessity. Likewise Paul's epistles were necessitated by his physical absence from the churches which needed his influence. Paul did not expect his letters to be collected or to be regarded as Holy Scripture. He wrote them to meet the local needs in his work of preaching the Gospel among the Greeks.

> That new loyalty to the inner life which Jesus had demanded, is seen at work in Paul. Upon some matters he spoke with what he felt to be the authority of the divine spirit. This was no mere manner of speaking with him, for he is sometimes very careful to absolve the spirit from responsibility for views which he himself held and recommended.[4]

In the earliest Gospel, Mark, Jesus appears as a commanding figure, filled with the Divine Spirit which made his teaching authoritative. Jesus says, ". . . all things must be fulfilled, which were written in the law of Moses, and in the prophets, and in

---

[3] E. F. Scott, *The Literature of the New Testament*, p. 8.
[4] Edgar J. Goodspeed, *The Formation of the New Testament*, p. 11; also read I Corinthians 7:25–26 and II Corinthians 11:17.

the psalms, concerning me."[5] This passage cannot be understood on any other supposition than that the writings of the New Testament furnish clear evidence to the tripartite division of the Hebrew canon of Scripture. Quotations are found in the New Testament from all of the books of the Old Testament except Obadiah, Nahum, Ezra, Nehemiah, Esther, Song of Songs, and Ecclesiastes.

The Christian church had, at the very beginning, a Bible, the canon of the Old Testament—or the Law, the Prophets, and the Writings (in the process of canonization)—and Apocrypha.

> When Jerome made his revision of the Latin Bible, toward the end of the fourth century, he put the books of the Greek Old Testament which were not in the Hebrew Bible in a group by themselves and called them the Apocrypha. The New Testament has no such appendix; there are, strictly speaking, no New Testament Apocrypha. But there are books not in our New Testament which at various times and in some localities have been considered part of it, and their temporary connection with it throws some light upon the way in which it was regarded. They formed a kind of fringe or border about the New Testament, the study of which is very instructive.[6]

The early church used the Septuagint (LXX), which is the Greek translation of the Hebrew Scriptures. The early Christians were taught to interpret the Septuagint as referring to Jesus as their Messiah. Early Christian worship was modeled on the worship of the synagogue. This worship consisted of prayer, the singing of a Psalm, reading from the Scripture, and lastly an address. When one of Paul's letters arrived, it would be read at the public meeting and would be substituted for the address. After Paul had been martyred his letters were listened to with more reverence. Gradually, instead of being substituted for the address, they took the place of the Scripture reading. Other

---

[5] Luke 24:44.
[6] Goodspeed, *op. cit.*, p. 157.

books, too, were read which had apostolic sanction. The question gradually grew in the minds of the early Christians, "What books should be included in the canon of the New Testament?" These books were selected by a gradual, tentative process, unconsciously by the mind of the church at large. Excluded books, such as the Epistle of Barnabas, the First Epistle of Clement and the Shepherd of Hermes, stand on a different plane from those books which were finally selected to make up our New Testament.

> Throughout the third century, "the New Testament" was a term to which no precise meaning could be attached. It was fully recognized that Christianity had its sacred book, worthy to be ranked with the Jewish Scriptures or even above them. But the limits of the Christian Bible were not defined, and as yet there was no central authority which could speak for the whole church and impose its judgment. The question as to which books should be included was left open, and different lists were drawn up by different outstanding teachers. On the principal books, all were agreed; but others were placed on a secondary list of "disputed books." The use of these was permitted for edification, but they were not to be regarded as in the full sense inspired. In course of time, this class of "disputed books" resolved itself into two—books which were not altogether certain and books which might be pretty confidently rejected. Those in the former division tended more and more to be frankly accepted while the others fell out altogether. It was not till after the middle of the fourth century that the New Testament took its definite form. In the year 367 A.D. Athanasius, who had come to be acknowledged as the foremost man in the whole church, issued his famous Easter letter, in which he enumerated the books as we now have them, and declared that these henceforth were to form the Christian Scriptures.[7]

---

[7] Scott, *op. cit.*, p. 291.

The canon of the New Testament was a gradual growth, just like the canon of the Old Testament. The New Testament was the result of Christian experience, recognized and formulated by the leading scholars of the universal church.[8] The Prophets and the Writings have the same relationship to the Law as the rest of the New Testament bears to the Gospels.

At one time it was thought that the early church developed peacefully. But from the very beginning the church was divided into parties, the Jewish and Gentile Christians, who were opposed to each other. Each of the New Testament writers maintains his own view of the Gospel. False teachings are spoken of in the later books, but the evidence which we have of these heretical views is vague and unsatisfactory. These writers assume that their audience is familiar with these views. The one thing that is clear to us, though, is that behind the New Testament is a controversial background. We know, too, that there were possible changes and additions to the New Testament as it stands today. The attitude of the early church toward some of the New Testament, at first, was similar to that toward hymns in our modern church worship.

> While using the hymns, the church has modified them from time to time, omitting and adding and rewriting so as to adapt them to new ideas and new moods of devotional feeling. In much the same manner, it dealt with the New Testament books.[9]

The collection of the Pauline letters led to a flood of other Christian letters, and the collection of the Four Gospels led to the writing of almost a score of later gospels. This secondary letter literature is given in the following table:[10]

---

[8] See *The Excluded Books of the New Testament*. Read J. A. Robinson, Introduction.

[9] Scott, *op. cit.*, p. 14.

[10] Edgar J. Goodspeed, *New Solutions of New Testament Problems* (Copyright 1927 by University of Chicago), p. 49; by permission.

A.D. 50–62	A.D. 70–90	A.D. 96–160
Paul's Letters:	Mark	Ephesians
Thessalonians I, II	Matthew	Revelation (7 letters)
Galatians	Luke–Acts	Hebrews
Corinthians I, II		I Peter
Romans		I Clement
Philippians		I John
Colossians		II John
Philemon		III John
		Ignatius, Ephesians
		Magnesians
		Trallians
		Romans
		Philadelphians
		Smyrneans
		Polycarp
		Polycarp, Philippians
		James
		Jude
		I Timothy
		II Timothy
		Titus
		Barnabas
		II Peter
		Epistle of Apostles
		Martyrdom of Polycarp

If one of the writings of the so-called Apostolic Fathers (I and II Clement, Ignatius, Barnabas, Hermas, and the Apostolic Decrees) had been taken into the canon, then, as a consequence of the length of these books the center of gravity of the New Testament would have been accompanied by relatively little increase of power and depth.[11]

The main divisions of the Christian church were formally in agreement as to the canon of the New Testament. The most influential of the Greek and Latin churches decided upon the twenty-seven books fixed by Athanasius in his letter in A.D. 367

---

[11] Dibelius, *op. cit.*, p. 23.

and included by Jerome in his revisions of the Latin Bible. The Syriac and Ethiopic New Testaments differ from both of these and differ still more from each other.

> We have no reason to believe that the canon of Rome differed materially from that of Cyprian at that time, as Africa probably derived her Christianity and everything connected with it directly from Italy. We should expect Spain to follow Africa, Gaul and Dalmatia to follow Rome, and that appears to be what happened.[12]
>
> So far as biblical books were concerned, individual churches were permitted to exercise their own discretion in the earliest centuries of the church. That a remarkable agreement of opinion was produced without any application of force is very significant. Something like a fixed canon had grown to have all the force of usage, and it was not till the second half of the fourth century that, from whatever cause or causes, this usage was stereotyped by various episcopal pronouncements made applicable to all the churches of a province or to the whole church catholic.[13]

The Council of Laodicea in A.D. 363 claims to have made the earliest conciliar list of Scripture books; however, the Council of Pope Damasus at Rome in A.D. 382 made another list. This is identical with Athanasius' list except that the Apocalypse is absent. In the Damasine Council of the Synod of 382 in Rome, Jerome was the leading spirit. We find in this list the same books given as in the Easter letter of Athanasius and in our modern Bibles, though there are differences in the order of the books. At the Council of Carthage in 397, Augustine was the leading spirit. In this council, as in the Damasine, the books as we have them in our New Testament are listed. With these two similar lists, backed by Jerome and Augustine, there could no longer be question of disagreement in the West.

---

[12] Alexander Souter, *The Text and Canon of the New Testament*, p. 189.
[13] *Ibid.*, p. 195.

· V ·

The Synoptic Gospels and Acts

The first four books of the New Testament, Matthew, Mark, Luke and John, are called Gospels, an English paraphrase of the Greek title of these books, *evangel*, which became the Anglo-Saxon *godspell*, which, in turn, was shortened into *gospel*. These books are biographies of Jesus, the first three of which are called "synoptic" because each gives a synopsis of Jesus' life. Mark's outline was used by the writers of Matthew and Luke. E. F. Scott says:

> The three Gospels of Matthew, Mark and Luke are independent works, and yet bear a very close relation to each other. They cover much the same ground; they give nearly the same selection of incidents; when one of them records a saying of Jesus, it is usually repeated in one or both of the others. . . . They not only agree in facts, but frequently in their very language, so that it is not uncommon to find whole sentences verbally the same. Not only so, but incidents and sayings which have no intrinsic connection are often placed in the same sequence by all three evangelists, proving that

they must have drawn from a common source. But while the agreements are striking, the differences are no less so. Again and again what is obviously the same incident is given in conflicting versions, or a saying of Jesus is reported in terms that are widely at variance. Why is it that the three writers who seem to be constantly using the same source are yet so independent? In almost every paragraph these two phenomena of agreement and difference are found together; on what theory of origin can we account for both of them? Here we have the synoptic problem, which has occupied many of the acutest minds for the best part of a century, and does not yet appear to be near a solution. Perhaps it will never be solved, for in some of its crucial aspects we have to deal with unknown quantities—documents that have now been lost and cannot be reconstructed except by doubtful inference. Of all literary problems this one which concerns the three Gospels is the most intricate and baffling, as it is incomparably the most important. Our knowledge of the life and work of Jesus is derived mainly from these Gospels, and the value of their testimony must depend on the conclusions we can form as to their origin.[1]

One of the sources from which our Gospels were derived was the Logia or the Sayings of Jesus in the Aramaic language. These sayings were probably written down by Matthew about A.D. 55 and were very soon translated into Greek for missionary use. The Logia is called by scholars Q, the first letter of the German word *Quelle*, meaning "source."[2] Other critics say that Q is a collection of some sayings of Jesus, the product of reminiscence and thoughtful recollection on the part of those who had heard Jesus speaking.

The relation of the three Gospels may be suggested by the following diagram.

[1] E. F. Scott, *The Literature of the New Testament*, pp. 21–22.
[2] See H. K. Booth, *The Background of the Bible*, p. 176.

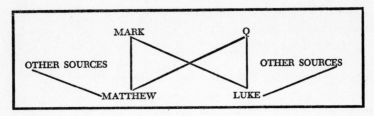

This device illustrates four points:

1. A comparison of Mark with Matthew and Luke shows like-
   nesses which can be explained only by assuming that Mark
   is the source of the other two.
2. Aside from the material drawn from Mark, Matthew and
   Luke have other material so much alike that it must have
   come from some common source.
3. There was probably more than one source common to Matthew and Luke so that, in the diagram, Q represents not a
   single source but several sources of which one very probably
   was the Logia of the Apostle Matthew.
4. Aside from the common source, Matthew and Luke each
   had independent sources not used by the other Gospel.[3]

MARK

When Peter met his death in Rome, Western Christianity
lost "its one great human document for the life of Jesus."[4] But
in Rome there lived a young man named Mark who translated
into Greek Peter's native Aramaic to the Roman Christians.
Mark had accompanied Paul and Barnabas to Cyprus on their
first missionary journey. He withdrew, however, from the party
when they landed in Pamphylia,[5] although he went on a second
missionary journey with Barnabas, who was his relative. In
Jerusalem, his mother's house was a center for the Christian
community. He was not only Peter's interpreter but his com-

---

[3] Wood and Grant, *The Bible as Literature*, pp. 233–34.
[4] Edgar J. Goodspeed, *The Story of the Bible*, p. 49.
[5] Acts 13:13; 15:37–40; Mark 1:14; 14:34–36.

panion. He realized how destitute the church would be if Peter's recollections of Jesus were not preserved.

At first this earliest Gospel was unwritten. The interpretation of the Law affected the first treatment of the memories of Jesus, whose sayings the early Jewish Christians preserved. This, naturally, gave rise to the oral Gospel.[6] Oral tradition was the prevailing form of the Gospel in the early years of the second century.

Mark's Gospel, then, was written to preserve Peter's recollections of Jesus, and this was the beginning of the Gospel-making movement. He was influenced by the conditions and needs of the Roman Christians for whom he wrote. It is Peter's picture of Jesus that Mark preserves for us. Jesus here appears as a commanding figure, filled with the divine spirit which made his teaching authoritative.

The Gospel of Mark was most probably composed in Rome, between A.D. 63 and 70. Critics determine this date from chapter 13, in which the end of the world is predicted. This chapter is intimately connected with the siege of Jerusalem; hence, the date cannot be far from A.D. 70.

The Gospel of Mark is famous for its swiftness, its vividness and its color. Mark supplements the known teaching matter of Jesus, such as the Sermon on the Mount. The first chapter shows us that Jesus was the popular hero in Galilee. Mark disposes of the baptism of Jesus and the temptation and comes quickly to the series of miracles. These dialogues show how opinion turned against Jesus, for at the close of chapter 1, Jesus, because of his popularity, could not enter the city openly, while at the end of chapter 6 the Pharisees took counsel against him. Mark discusses the attitude of the different parties toward Jesus, and this discussion is followed by the parable section.

A new section begins with chapter 8, in which Jesus is revealed as the Messiah. Chapter 10 begins with the Jerusalem journey, while chapters 14 and 15 are the Passion stories, showing that all the disciples forsook Jesus and fled, except Peter,

---

[6] I Corinthians 11–15; Acts 20:35.

who later denied him. Chapter 16 begins with the Resurrection story but breaks off abruptly. Scholars tell us that the loss of the original ending was due to dilapidation,[7] just as most papyrus rolls have lost by constant use either one end or both ends. Critics feel that some editor substituted the last twelve verses for the original ending of Mark and that the original ending described a Galilean reappearance of Jesus. This account is preserved in the conclusion of Matthew. These last twelve verses are found in no early manuscript. Even in later manuscripts they appear in several diverse forms.

> Informal and unambitious as Mark's Gospel narrative is, lightly as it was esteemed in the ancient church in comparison with the richer works of Matthew and Luke, no more convincing or dramatic account has been written of the sublime and heroic effort of Jesus to execute the greatest task ever conceived by man—to set up the Kingdom of God on earth.[8]

Though Mark's Gospel is the oldest, it is itself a combination of several earlier documents. Mark wished to supersede the imperfect records which were in use at that time. Aside from Peter's reminiscences and the sayings (source usually designated by the symbol Q), Mark also had an extended account of the Passion story. These are the three sources which he used for his Gospel. He combined the Passion story with Jesus' ministry which had led up to it. "In the ancient words of Papias, Mark was intent on one thing only, to omit or falsify none of the things that he had heard."[9]

MATTHEW

Matthew was very likely intended for Jewish converts; it depicts Jesus as the Messiah and the King, as the fulfiller of

---

[7] See Edgar J. Goodspeed, *New Solutions of New Testament Problems*, pp. 116 f.

[8] Edgar J. Goodspeed, *The Story of the New Testament*, p. 53.

[9] Scott, *op. cit.*, p. 64.

the law and the highest expectations of the Jewish nation. Most modern scholars are inclined to believe that the Gospel of Matthew is not a translation from the Aramaic but that it was written in Greek by Matthew himself about A.D. 80, or perhaps as late as A.D. 95. The sources of Matthew are Mark and Q (the Sayings of Jesus) and other sources. The aim of Matthew's Gospel was to interweave with Mark's sketch of Jesus' life a large part of Jesus' Sayings which were current in the church, most of which were found in the "Sayings, Source Q." Matthew, then, rather than Mark, became a substitute for the oral tradition, which was dying out.

Matthew, one of the twelve disciples, buttressed the work of Jesus with Old Testament quotations. Matthew also took over all of Mark except perhaps forty verses.[10] The original conclusion of Mark can perhaps be found in Matthew 28:9–10 and 16–20. Though Matthew is neither the oldest nor the most beautiful, it is the most important Gospel because of its systematic arrangement and because it contains the fullest account of Jesus' teaching. It is also the most comprehensive Gospel, and it commended itself to the church because the church was constantly in the writer's mind. The author wished to see the different bodies of Christians united in a common loyalty to Jesus, and it is this catholicity of spirit that made Matthew the representative Gospel.

Tradition and some of the modern scholars ascribe the authorship of this Gospel to Matthew, but E. F. Scott thinks that it belongs to a time when Matthew must have been long dead. However, Matthew might have drawn up a document which served as the nucleus of the later work.[11] The late date given (of somewhere between A.D. 80–95) is determined by the fact that persecution was not a serious factor in the church until near the end of the first century. Our knowledge of Palestinian Christianity, during the years after the destruction of Jerusalem, comes from this Gospel. Temple ritual had been brought to an

---

[10] See Edgar J. Goodspeed, *New Solutions of New Testament Problems,* p. 116.

[11] See Scott, *op. cit.,* p. 67.

end; hence, the purpose of the author was to show that Jesus was the fulfiller of the Jewish law and prophecy.

The Gospel of Mark was a new type in the extant literature written by men of the Jewish race.[12] In Matthew, however, the Gospel had developed into a distinct literary form, different from anything that had preceded it, yet in the historical literature of Israel there are literary ancestors of Mark and Matthew.

Israel's historical literature began with biographical writing, as is shown in Samuel and Kings in the stories of Saul, David and Solomon. Later, Elijah was the hero of a collection of narratives. None of these came down to us as separate books, but rather in the form of compilations.

The books of the prophets are similar to the Gospels in that they are a record of the deeds and sayings of one central character. As in the time of Jesus, the sayings of each prophet were gathered together and compiled after the prophet's death. Hence we see not only that the books of the Old Testament were compilations but also that Matthew, Mark, and Luke are compilations from earlier documents.

> In the two-volume work Luke–Acts we have a writing which is Gentile-Christian both in authorship and destination. Consonant with this is the individual literary consciousness of the author, in contrast to the communal character which we considered in connection with the Gospel of Matthew. It is a striking fact, however, that despite the author's familiarity with the form of Greek historical writing, his method of composition is far more Jewish than Greek. Were we to take into account only the way in which the book is compiled from earlier writings, we might be tempted to believe the compiler to have been a Jew rather than a Greek. The mastery of the Greek language, the use of the Greek mode of introduction and dedication, and even the conscious historico-literary ideal of learning the

---

[12] See H. T. Fowler, *The History and Literature of the New Testament,* pp. 319 f.

course of things accurately from the best witnesses and then writing them in order, seem acquisitions more probable for a cultured Hellenistic Jew than the Jewish mode of compilation for a Greek.[13]

LUKE

Very likely neither Matthew nor Luke had seen the other's Gospel; hence, they cannot be placed very far apart in time. Luke was written after the siege of Jerusalem in A.D. 70, for Luke speaks of "Jerusalem compassed with armies."[14] Critics, therefore, place this Gospel between the years A.D. 80 and 100. Luke, like Matthew, uses for his main sources Mark and Q; and in addition he has a larger amount of material from other sources than Matthew, and this material is grouped under L, or Luke's special source. Luke also had the oral Gospel, and perhaps Matthew's Aramaic Gospel.

The L material is homogeneous in style and in vocabulary. It is a collection of all the saying and acts of Jesus and also the Passion narrative. It forms an orderly sequence and is a small gospel in itself. It is southern Palestinian rather than Galilean, especially the Resurrection narratives. The structure of Luke, then, is nearly two-fifths Mark, one-fifth Q, and three-fifths L,[15] and the purpose is to give a record of the life of Jesus and to weave together these various sources.

Luke is spoken of as "the beloved physician," for he discloses his profession in his use of technical terms in describing diseases.[16] The style of Luke suggests some Hellenic center, for it is artistic and is written in purer Greek than the other Gospels.

It is this historical aim that leads Luke to fix the date of Jesus' birth by the Augustan enrollment under Quirinius, to date the appearance of John the Baptist

---

[13] Fowler, *op. cit.*, pp. 331–32; reprinted by permission of the publisher, the Macmillan Company.

[14] Luke 21:20.

[15] See Scott, *op. cit.*, p. 83.

[16] Luke 4:23; 22:44; Acts 3:7,9,18; 12:23; 28:5.

in the fifteenth year of Tiberius, and to tell how old
Jesus was when he commenced to preach. He is the
only writer in the New Testament who sees the need
of such particulars and tries to supply them.[17]

Luke was dissatisfied with fragmentary gospels of his day;
hence he used, as no other writer of the New Testament, his
source material critically. Like European authors, he had a
literary patron, Theophilus. Luke comes to us complete, without
any late additions or editorial revisions, from the author himself.

Luke and Matthew prefix to Mark's narrative the beautiful
story of the Nativity; yet each of the two writers uses a different source for Jesus' birth and childhood. Luke, like Matthew, follows Mark and Q in disclosing the public ministry of
Jesus. Luke does not, like Matthew, interpret Jesus as the
Messiah fulfilling the Law and the Prophets. But he presents
Jesus in the true biographical way—as he was in both deed and
word. We are indebted to Luke for the seven distinct occasions
on which Jesus prayed during the critical times of his life. We
are also indebted to Luke for the great hymns of the church,
the Gloria in Excelsis, the Magnificat, the Benedictus and the
Nunc Dimittis. Luke also gave recognition to the freedom of
association between men and women.

Luke was a Gentile and a Greek, writing for Gentiles and
calling attention to the significance of Jesus for the Roman
world. Because of Luke's long association with Paul, we find
that he portrays the universal nature of Jesus and of Christianity. He writes in the spirit of Jesus' charity, tolerance and
catholicity. Luke was probably a native of Antioch or of
Philippi, and he probably met Paul first at Troas. "Luke was the
cultured Greek who found in life the teachings of Jesus universal
God and universal man."[18]

ACTS

Before we discuss the fourth Gospel, John, we shall consider

---

[17] Edgar J. Goodspeed, *The Story of the New Testament*, pp. 67–68.
[18] Fowler, *op. cit.*, p. 348.

the second part of the third Gospel, which is called the Acts of the Apostles. This book, like Luke, is dedicated to Theophilus and was written by Luke, but it is less bound to the fixed tradition already known to the churches. Acts is even more literary than Luke.

> Those who assume that their author made use of the Jewish historian Josephus in Acts must place them at earliest in the last decade of the first century.[19]

Luke and Acts must be taken together for a right estimate of the purpose as well as for date and authorship. The purpose of Acts is to show the result of Jesus' spirit animating the apostles in their founding of the churches, and also to show the progress of the Greek mission. Acts was written in the lifetime of Paul, presumably during his Roman imprisonment.[20] Acts presents us with the vital conception "that the work of the church is a continuation of Christ's energy."[21] The date of Acts is not much later than that of the Gospel of Luke, for he refers to the Gospel as "the former treatise."[22]

The Gospel of Luke and the Acts of the Apostles are one continuous work divided into two parts. A papyrus roll was not to exceed a certain length, and we see that Luke, who wrote the two longest books in the New Testament, put the greatest amount he could into both rolls. He doubtless had much more material on the life and Sayings of Jesus and the apostles than he was actually able to use.

Acts is in two parts, the first of which closes with Acts 15:35. That Luke used a written source is shown by the marked difference between the Greek style of the first fifteen chapters and that of the second part beginning with Acts 15:36. The sources generally accepted are the Jerusalem A source from Acts 3:1—

---

[19] Martin Dibelius, *A Fresh Approach to the New Testament and Early Christian Literature*, p. 65.

[20] See Edgar J. Goodspeed, *New Solutions of New Testament Problems*, p. 94.

[21] J. Moffatt, *Introduction to the Literature of the New Testament*, p. 285.

[22] Acts 1:1.

5:16 (the church at Jerusalem was headed by Peter and John);
the Jerusalem B source for Acts 2 and Acts 5:17–42; the Jerusalem C source for Acts 8:5–40, 9:31–11:18, and 12:1–24; the
Antioch source for Acts 6:1–8:4, 11:19–30, and 12:25–15:35;
and the Pauline source for Acts 9:1–30. The second part of Acts
contains the four passages in the "we" sections: Acts 16:10–17;
Acts 20:5–15; Acts 21:1–18; and Acts 27:1–28.

We see, then, that in the book of Acts, as in the Gospel of
Luke, a method of compilation has been followed. The parallel
sections of the book of Acts are explained by the use of two
documents, describing the same event, yet in partial conflict
with each other.

> All the documents that went to the making of Acts
> have disappeared and nothing can be said about them
> that is not mere conjecture.[23]

Luke edited these sources as he thought best, and because
of his skill he became the first of church historians.

> The traditions of stories and words accessible to the
> evangelists were sufficient for describing the work of
> Jesus; but for depicting the gradual growth of the
> church, the new foundations, the organizations, its
> penetration into the world—for all these purposes the
> known apostolic legends were very insufficient sources.
> Faced with such a problem, the writer could not be a
> mere collector; he must in this case be an author. He
> attempted to satisfy this requirement, and as a conse-
> quence the Acts of the Apostles became the most lit-
> erary book in the New Testament.[24]

The author of Acts follows the usual custom of Greek and
Jewish writers and, either with or without knowledge of the
particular situation, describes both the attitude of mind and the
preaching of the earliest Christian witnesses in the way he
imagines them. Acts was intended to describe the progress of

---

[23] E. F. Scott, *op. cit.*, p. 104.
[24] Dibelius, *op. cit.*, pp. 261–62.

the Gospel from Jerusalem to Rome, and the author shows the power of the Christian spirit with which the persons in the narrative are charged. This putting together of sources and traditions signifies a long stride in the evolution of primitive Christian literature. Acts describes the work of Peter and Paul and shows the emancipation of Christianity from its Judaic origin. It also shows the origin and progress of the religion of Jesus, and it emphasizes the unity of the church. Three-sixths of Acts is devoted to Paul, two-sixths to Peter, and one-sixth to the other apostles.

The spread of the Gospel from Jerusalem to Rome may be sketched under a few main divisions:

1. Early days of the church in Jerusalem (1–7).
2. Spread through Palestine to Phoenicia, Cyprus, and Antioch (8–12).
3. Advance through Cyprus to central Asia Minor (13–14).
4. Official recognition at Jerusalem of Gentile Christianity (15).
5. Advance to Macedonia and Achaia (14–18:22).
6. The great Ephesus Mission (18:23–21:16).
7. Check through arrest in Jerusalem and imprisonment in Caesarea (21:17–26:30).
8. Advance to Rome (27–28).[25]

This brief summary, however, does not do justice to the character sketches and the picturesque narrative out of which this biographical history springs, for throughout the book we feel ourselves in contact with the real persons and with genuine incidents.

The Synoptic Gospels and Acts do not show a direct influence of the letters of Paul. Had the writer of Acts been acquainted with Paul's letters, surely he would have used them to enrich his story of Paul's work. But after Acts, every book of the New Testament shows the influence of the letters of Paul.

---

[25] Fowler, *op. cit.*, p. 352; reprinted by permission of the Macmillan Company.

• VI •

The Johannine Writings

Five new Testament writings are ascribed, by tradition, to the Apostle John—the Fourth Gospel, the book of Revelation, and the First, Second, and Third Epistles of John.

> A manuscript of part of the New Testament believed to date back to about 100 A.D. . . . has been found in a collection of ancient papyri in the Rylands Museum at Manchester. . . . Written in Greek, it consists of a part of the Gospel of St. John and may upset previous theories of biblical scholars about the order in which various gospels were set down. . . . The manuscript measures 3½ by 2½ inches. On one side are John 18:31, 33, telling of the appearance of Christ before Pilate. On the other side are John 18:37, 38.[1]

Critics agree that the Johannine problem is more baffling than the Synoptic problem. Not until the nineteenth century was it thought that the Gospel of John was anonymous. Toward the end of the nineteenth century, scholars held that the Fourth Gospel was a work of late origin. In the twentieth century this

---

[1] The Tulsa *Tribune*, Nov. 23, 1936, p. 1.

view is no longer maintained. The Gospel was introduced into the world of that extra-Christian movement which we call Gnosticism.

> References to the Gospel can be discovered in the literature of about 150 A.D., and it seems to have been known in Gnostic circles as early as 130 A.D., and must then have been for some time in circulation. On the other hand it can hardly have been written before the close of the first century, for the author shows acquaintance with the Gospel of Luke, which has to be dated about 90 A.D. It must, therefore, be assigned to some date between 95 and 115 A.D., and most probably belongs to the first decade of the second century. All the peculiarities of its teaching are found, on closer examination, to fit in with its origin about that time.[2]

THE GOSPEL OF JOHN

The Gospel of John was written after the fall of Jerusalem that was prophesied by Jesus. We feel that the author of this Gospel is a Palestinian Jewish Christian and that he wrote to correct, interpret and supplement the Synoptic narratives.

> In addition to his early experience with Jesus this evangelist knew the Gospel of Mark and probably the other Synoptics, also was familiar with some of the loftiest thought of Paul as we know it in Romans, I Corinthians, and Ephesians and probably with I Peter too.[3]

John restates Christian truth in Greek terms. The Fourth Gospel begins with the doctrine of incarnation as conceived by Paul and formulated under the Logos theory. John calls Jesus the Logos, the Word or the Thought of God. The Jewish philosopher Philo had already identified the revealing Word of Jehovah with the Logos of Greek thought.

---

[2] E. F. Scott, *The Literature of the New Testament*, p. 235.
[3] See H. von Soden, *Urchristliche Literaturgeschichte*, Eng. trans., p. 424.

This central personality of the book is conceived as an
eternal Being who is identified with the world-principle
called the Word which was in the beginning with God
and by which all things have been made. First, he
existed before his earthly career, for he was in the
beginning with God. Second, he became flesh and
dwelt among us. Third, he survived death, and is represented among his disciples by his Spirit, who reveals
the things of the Christ to believers. The main body of
the Gospel consists of the explanations and proofs that
Jesus Christ is this Being, the eternal Word, and of the
contents of the Christ with the opposition. John the
Baptist testified that Jesus was the Christ, and Jesus
himself by action and discussion makes the claim con-
tinuously from the beginning of the book.[4]

John's purpose is to interpret Jesus' deeds as signs of his
Divinity, and also to emphasize the Divinity of his character
and personality, independent of his works. The author is so
steeped in Hellenistic ideas that his personal knowledge of God
clothes itself in these terms. Through Jesus he has known God,
and through Jesus he has obtained knowledge that transcends
all existence. This knowledge is not that of the ordinary Gnostics, for John obtains his insight directly. While opposing
Gnosticism, the writer sympathizes with some of its positions,
so much so that it has both in ancient and modern times been
ascribed to Gnostic authorship. John's answer to the Gnostic
teachers of his day is that God may be known through mystical
contemplation, but only so when God is first known through
Jesus.

He believes, then, that in Christ there has been given
a twofold revelation. God is at once the righteous God
of whom the prophets had spoken, and the absolute
being for whom the Greeks had been seeking, ever
since the days of Plato.[5]

---

[4] Wood and Grant, *The Bible as Literature*, p. 263.
[5] E. F. Scott, *The New Testament Idea of Revelation*, p. 194.

After the prologue, no further direct reference is made to the Logos doctrine. In the body of the Gospel *glory* takes the place of *Logos*. The author, like Paul, falls back on the Old Testament idea of the glory of God. The Synoptic Gospels described Jesus as Prophet and Teacher. The Fourth Gospel, however, answers the question which arises out of the Synoptic Gospels: What was it in Jesus that gave authority to his teachings? In the life of Jesus, John sees the divine—the light of the world—and this inward knowledge is only possible through knowledge of the actual life of Christ. The first three Gospels relate the ministry and the Person of Jesus, while the Fourth Gospel presents the trancendent Personality and shows the significance of the historical facts. The purpose is clearly stated at the close of the Gospel: ". . . these are written, that ye might believe that Jesus is the Christ, the Son of God; and that believing ye may have life through his name."[6]

After this closing statement, an appendix or epilogue was added by the editors in which it is stated that the beloved disciple wrote the Gospel, but the disciple is never named. Whoever this beloved disciple was, his semi-independent Gospel grew alongside the Synoptic account. This Gospel seems to have centered around a particular circle of believers who preserved the nucleus which resulted in the Fourth Gospel. The traditional opinion was that this book was written at Ephesus and was the work of the Apostle John in his old age. The problem of authorship is unsettled, yet the earliest editors feel as the church, throughout the ages, has felt, that the author of the Fourth Gospel understood Jesus best because he was spiritually closest to him.

> Although the composite authorship of the Gospel cannot be admitted, it contains at least two passages which were not in the original work. One of them is that closing chapter, which was added by the early editors. In itself the chapter is one of the most exquisite in the New Testament, but it is different in character from the

---

[6] John 20:31.

rest of the Gospel. The story of the risen Christ appearing to his disciples at the lake of Galilee may be compared to Luke's account of the journey to Emmaus, and is possibly drawn from the same source. It may be conjectured that the editors, wishing to add a final chapter, availed themselves of one of the traditions which the synoptic writers had omitted, and which they wished to preserve for its own sake. Into this story they weave their testimony as to the authorship of the Gospel by the Beloved Disciple. The other extraneous passage is that concerning the woman taken in adultery (8:1–11). In the oldest manuscripts this passage is wanting, and in others it is marked as doubtful, or assigned to a different place or to another Gospel altogether. The best modern editions of the Greek text print it by itself, at the end of the Gospels. In this passage also we are to see a stray fragment of tradition which the church was unwilling to lose. Possibly it had been handed down by word of mouth; more likely it had a place in one of the early documents which had gone to the making of the Synoptic Gospels. Why it had been left out from Matthew and Luke we cannot tell; but though it has no right to stand in the Fourth Gospel, we may be grateful to the early editors who inserted it, and thus preserved for us a priceless addition to our records of the life of Christ.[7]

John's spiritual Gospel is subjective as opposed to the objective Synoptics. Because it was written in the Greek world where there was intellectual opposition to Christianity, this book breathes the spirit of contest and debate. It combines both Greek philosophy and Hebrew structure, for its style is antithetical. The Fourth Gospel transplanted Christianity into Greek soil and its message into Greek terms. This Gospel came into competition with the Synoptics and with their Jewish way of presenting Christianity. However, a few years after the appear-

[7] E. F. Scott, *Literature of the New Testament*, pp. 258–59.

ance of John it was combined with the Synoptic Gospels into the fourfold Gospel.

> So while we find Paul, Clement, and Polycarp using the oral gospel; Matthew and Luke using Mark; Ignatius, Barnabas and the Teaching of the Twelve Apostles using Matthew, and Marcion using Luke, most of the books written toward the middle of the second century or soon after it show acquaintance with the fourfold gospel.[8]

The four Gospels were not collected and put forth together as authorities, but they were not long in coming to be so regarded. They were read in Christian meetings side by side with the Greek translations of the Jewish Bible. They had become a unit, and there was no thought of choosing between them. The fourfold Gospel became the cornerstone of the New Testament.

REVELATION

The church, as well as Judaism, availed itself of apocalyptic literature. The Jewish apocalyptic writings, of which Daniel is the best example, served as a model for the book of Revelation. Because of the persecutions of the Christians, the church needed the encouragement which the book of Revelation was able to furnish. The Jewish apocalyptic writings help us to understand the symbolism in Revelation because they served as models for this book.

> The secrets that it [Revelation] contains are mainly of the nature of historical puzzles. . . . In its present form, it bears all the marks of unity. Its various parts all fit together and it advances toward a great climax with real dramatic power. But there are many indications that this unity has been imposed on a number of documents which were originally separate and which were drawn up at different times and in different circumstances. The sifting of these diverse sources of the

---

[8] Edgar J. Goodspeed, *The Formation of the New Testament*, p. 37.

book has given rise to critical questions of much complexity, which have not yet by any means been answered.[9]

In this new type of Christian literature is shown the welding of the new prophetic sense with the old Jewish idea of inspired books. In Revelation, Jesus appears to the prophet and dictates the letters to the churches. Hence there is complete continuity from Abraham's time to the Christian era, for the twelve stars in Revelation represent the twelve tribes of Israel, and Israel brings forth the Messiah, common to Jewish writings.

Revelation was compiled to sustain the church under its new conditions, brought about by the enforcement of Caesar-worship in the reign of Domitian, about the year A.D. 95. The Christians refused to observe this cult and were therefore persecuted. John, who had been exiled to the island of Patmos, writes to the seven churches most gravely affected. He wishes to show the real significance of good and evil in the world; hence he writes in alternating pictures of light and darkness, of heaven and hell. He wishes, also, to present the significance of emperor-worship and shows how Rome is to be destroyed by an earthquake and by fire.[10] Revelation forecasts events which are to happen in the future and describes beforehand events which took place in A.D. 70 and the years immediately preceding, and it is concerned with the fall of Jerusalem and Judaism in 70 and the setting up of Christ's Spiritual Kingdom, the New Jerusalem.[11]

Revelation was written about A.D. 96 by one who calls himself John. Heretofore, prophecies were written under names of revered men of the past, such as the apocalypses of Enoch, Baruch, Moses, Isaiah and Daniel. We know that John the disciple was interested in apocalyptic literature. If Revelation is by the same author as the Fourth Gospel, it was written earlier, because it contains many Hebrew idioms as compared with the purer Greek of the Fourth Gospel. Critics try to prove that the

---

[9] E. F. Scott, *The Literature of the New Testament*, p. 276.
[10] Revelation 17:16.
[11] Revelation 21.

author of the Fourth Gospel could not have written Revelation by the following fact:

> Although this book claimed to be by John, and is known to the early church from the second century onward, yet its admission to the canon was in doubt and dispute for centuries. Had it been unquestionably from John the Apostle, it seems impossible that it should not have been admitted speedily into the canon.[12]

Revelation is built around the letters to the seven churches, the Messianic woes, the antichrist who is conceived as Nero and the New Jerusalem. The book is an expression of supreme faith before those who were bent on crushing the church. It is an expression of faith in God, in Jesus, and in the spiritual over the material. Revelation consists entirely of visions and prophecies.

> For the primitive church the Spirit was manifest in miracles and speaking with tongues. The seer of the Apocalypse attributed his strange visions to the Spirit, and his work is still known, pre-eminently, as "the Revelation."[13]

I, II, AND III JOHN

The three epistles of John are pastoral epistles dealing with and refuting Gnosticism in general. I John answers the Gnostic heresies concerning the dual nature of Christ. It implies facts which the Fourth Gospel states as historically true. Critics agree because of the style, vocabulary, and type of thought that I John and the Fourth Gospel were written by the same author. I John is superior to II and III John. It is subjective, and the probable date of composition is between A.D. 95 and 115, at Ephesus.

Both II John and III John are examples of private correspondence and were nearly rejected from the Canon because of their obvious inferiority. The two letters were probably written at the same time, for II John 12–13 is almost identical with

---

[12] H. K. Booth, *The Background of the Bible*, p. 187.
[13] E. F. Scott, *The New Testament Idea of Revelation*, p. 242.

III John 13–14. The author calls himself "the elder." This title was assumed by the older teachers who, in a direct manner, linked themselves with the apostles. II John is addressed to the "elect lady," perhaps symbolically representing the church, and states that the true Christian life is grounded in its love for Christ. III John is addressed to Gaius, yet both Diotrephes and Demetrius are mentioned, which help to authenticate the book. Though these two letters were slow in obtaining a place in the New Testament canon, their historical interest has recently been recognized.

> It consists chiefly in this, that they afford us a vivid glimpse into the momentous change from the primitive apostolic ministry to the episcopal system. Hitherto the church has been controlled by itinerant missionaries, whose authority depended on the "spiritual gifts" with which they were endowed. In place of this original form of government, there gradually arose a local, official ministry, and the two epistles come to us from the very time when this transition was in process.[14]

---

[14] E. F. Scott, *The Literature of the New Testament*, p. 269.

• VII •

Miscellaneous Letters

JUDE

Jude, classed among the general epistles, is concerned with the virulent type of Gnosticism. Jude is annoyed by the Gnostics and condemns merely professional Christianity. We know the author of Jude through his work, through the fact that he bore the common name of Jude and had a brother who bore the common name of James. Jude quotes from the Jewish apocalyptic books, placing them on the same level with the Old Testament. Though Jude contains little of religious value, yet the remarkably beautiful doxology is one of the most cherished utterances of the New Testament:

> Now unto him that is able to keep you from falling, and to present you faultless before the presence of his glory with exceeding joy, to the only wise God our Saviour, be glory and majesty, dominion and power, both now and ever. Amen.[1]

---

[1] Jude 24–25.

II PETER

II Peter, another general epistle, is really a revision of the Epistle of Jude. Its date is assigned to about A.D. 150, and it serves as a bridge between the New Testament and the literature of the succeeding age. The authorship was formerly ascribed to the Apostle Peter, but evidence that Peter did not write this epistle is overwhelming. Both Jude and II Peter are concerned with teachers who claim to be Christian, yet are unorthodox. II Peter is, like Jude, an appeal for practical holiness and a plea against Gnosticism. It was written to confirm a particular position of Christian faith—the hope of the second coming of Christ. The second chapter not only reproduces Jude's ideas, but reproduces his words and phrases. It is written in Attic Greek and has had a place in the New Testament since the Council of Laodicea in A.D. 372. These two short letters bring us to the end of the New Testament period. "... we ... look for new heavens and a new earth, wherein dwelleth righteousness."[2]

I PETER

I Peter, another general epistle, written in the best Hellenistic Greek of the New Testament, is filled with Pauline language and Pauline thought. It is written to the Christian churches in Pontus, Galatia, Cappadocia, Asia, and Bithynia and speaks to the Christians who were being persecuted, probably at the end of Domitian's reign. I Peter is a letter of hope, as Paul's are letters of faith.

The author of this letter advises the Christians in Asia Minor, even though there were persecutions, to accept graciously the provisions of the government under which they lived, just as Christ offered no resistance to those who caused his suffering.[3]

This epistle seems to have been written from Rome. The attributing of the authorship of this letter to the Apostle Peter

---

[2] II Peter 3:13.
[3] I Peter 2:22.

must have come much later than its writing. Great names were often attached to Christian writings by those who collected them. Peter, according to tradition, perished in Nero's massacre. Peter the Galilean could not have written the excellent Greek of this epistle, yet he may have had a scribe write for him, for he says: "By Sylvanus, a faithful brother . . . I have written briefly."[4]

HEBREWS

In the Epistle to the Hebrews the Christians were counseled to meet the persecutions of the Roman Empire by building an inner world of thought.

The latter part of the first century found the church in conflict with the government under which it lived. From the beginning, its life had been complicated by adjustment to and interference from various official groups. Jewish religious leaders had opposed Jesus, and finally brought about his death. Jewish unfriendliness, appealing to Roman authorities, had brought frequent difficulty to the life of the early church. Paul was repeatedly brought before both Jewish and Roman tribunals, and finally met his death, we believe, as did Peter also, when Nero took action against the church in Rome. Other leaders of the Christian movement, such as James and Stephen, had suffered martyrdom. But previous to the reign of the Emperor Domitian, there had been no consistent policy of the government to persecute Christians as such. Jewish opposition had been sporadic, occasional, and unregulated,—governed rather by individual, personal feeling or by mob action than by official policy. On the Roman side, even Nero's persecution, brutal though it was, did not threaten the life of the church at large. It was confined to the City of Rome, and was occasioned rather by caprice than by any considered policy of opposition to the group's ac-

---

[4] I Peter 5:12.

tivities. . . . According to Tacitus, the Christians were fraudulently charged with setting fire to the City, and the motive of the charge was to deflect the blame from Nero himself. . . . At the end of the first century, conditions were much more serious for the church as a whole, for the persecution under the Emperor Domitian was due to a deliberate policy and was not confined to any one city or area. . . . Three books in the New Testament reflect this situation in the reign of Domitian when the Empire and the church came into conflict: Hebrews, First Peter, and Revelation.[5]

Hebrews, the earliest of these three works, is philosophical, orderly in development of thought, and dignified in its language, and is, therefore, more consciously a work of literature than any other New Testament book. We do not know the author of Hebrews, or where it was written. The early collectors of Christian literature ascribe this book to Paul, but the thought and style are not Paul's, and it is later than Paul's time; hence, the writer is unknown. It is thought that the epistle, which is really a sermon, was connected with Rome, for Clement of Rome, who wrote as early as A.D. 96, quotes from it. Critics, therefore, date it between A.D. 80 and 90.

> The whole historic religious system of Judaism, with its scriptures, its sacrifices, its prophets, its succession of heroes, its doctrines, its priesthood, and its promises, give only a partial revelation. Even angels could not do what Jesus had done. . . . In Jesus, God had given the very reality itself.[6]

The author of Hebrews was influenced by a school of philosophy in Alexandria, the leader of whom was Philo, a Hellenistic Jew. He blended Plato's philosophy with Jewish religious thought in an attempt to find the Platonic doctrines implicit in

---

[5] Mary Ely Lyman, *The Christian Epic*, pp. 169–71.
[6] Lyman, *op. cit.*, p. 177.

Hebrew Scripture. The Fourth Gospel, also, made use of this philosophy.

The unknown author of Hebrews makes it clear that Christianity is the perfect type of religion and that worship will rekindle, in the Christians of the third generation, the awe which the Gospel had once inspired. Christianity, he says, has brought fulfilment to Judaism because Judaism was given by God. Christianity had carried to fruition what was in the mind of God from the beginning. The death of Christ made him our High Priest.

> The author declares (and this is the pervading idea of the book) that through Christ we are enabled to grasp the reality of things which have been hitherto known only in their dim reflection.[7]

Pauline thought and Greek philosophy joined hands in Hebrews. Paul's letters, Hebrews, and the Fourth Gospel illustrate, in the order named, the development through fifty years of Christian interpretation, especially in the Gentile field.

> The deeply spiritual gospel of Paul was developed by Greek Christianity to the positions revealed to us in Hebrews and the Fourth Gospel. . . . According to Hebrews, faith is a firm conviction, an assurance, to which one holds unswervingly, of the verity of the unseen or spiritual realities. Thus its intellectual side is emphasized more in Paul. In the eleventh chapter of Hebrews the examples cited would almost allow our defining faith as unshakable confidence in God. But with Paul faith consists essentially of personal union with Christ.[8]

---

[7] Scott, *op. cit.*, p. 205.
[8] Wood and Grant, *The Bible as Literature*, pp. 315–16.

· VIII ·

Paul's Letters

Paul's letters must have, by the time of the writing of II Peter, been gathered into a collection, for his letters are spoken of and are regarded with special reverence:

> . . . even as our beloved brother Paul also according to the wisdom given unto him hath written unto you; as also in all his epistles, speaking in them of these things; in which are some things hard to be understood, which they that are unlearned and unstable wrest, as they do also the other scriptures, unto their own destruction.[1]

Critics speak of Paul's thirteen letters as I Thessalonians, Galatians, I Corinthians, II Corinthians, Romans, Philippians, Philemon, II Thessalonians, Ephesians, Colossians, I Timothy, II Timothy and Titus. The last three, in their present form, cannot be regarded as Paul's. About the authorship of II Thessalonians and Ephesians critics differ. Most of the critics, however, assign, with reasonable certainty, the first seven letters listed above to Paul.

The earliest New Testament writings which have come down

---

[1] II Peter 3:15–16.

to us in their original form are the letters of Paul. Letters were not a new literary form among the Greeks. Plato's letters are quoted by Plutarch and Cicero. Epicurus' letters were well known the century before Christ. Paul's First Epistle to the Thessalonians, the earliest in date of the New Testament books, was written about A.D. 53. It is the oldest Christian writing which survives.

We have a definite historical record of Paul's work for seventeen years after his conversion. In Damascus, he worked for three years, and in Tarsus and Antioch and the region between, he worked for fourteen years. In Macedonia, Greece, and Asia Minor he established a Christian church in each important center. When he left these churches, he kept in touch with them through his letters, which gradually took on the form of Scripture.

I THESSALONIANS

I Thessalonians and Galatians were written on Paul's second missionary journey, when he was about fifty, to reassure the leaders of those churches and to clarify his teachings concerning the second coming of Christ. At this time Paul was just beginning his work at Corinth. With the greatest of care, he dictated these letters to someone who happened to be with him, adding his words of personal greeting and the signature.

Into the Book of Acts we can fit Paul's writings, for he speaks for himself in this book. His letters cover about ten years of his missionary work, which lasted for thirty years. After the Council in Jerusalem in A.D. 49, Paul began a Gentile mission on a larger scale than hitherto attempted. On this second missionary journey he retraced his first journey in Asia Minor. He founded the church at Philippi, and then went to Thessalonica and to Corinth. He left Corinth to visit Jerusalem and Antioch, and after a year, he went to Ephesus, where he remained for three years. He went back to Jerusalem, the Jewish stronghold, where he was mobbed in the Temple, and was kept prisoner for two years at Caesarea. He was sent to Rome for two years,[2]

---

[2] Acts 28:30–51.

but at this point the record ceases and we have only conjecture.

Paul had been expelled from Thessalonica because a large number of the heathen who had accepted the Jewish faith were attracted to his new teaching about Christ. He had left Thessalonica only a few months after he had established the church there, and he wrote these letters because he felt that a persecution similar to his would be directed against them. Paul also wished to remove the concern about some members of the church who had recently died. He urges the belief in the second coming of Christ and shares in these letters the apocalyptic idea of the visible return of Jesus. II Thessalonians depicts the dæmonic antichrist and urges the Christians not to cease work because of the near end of the world.

II Thessalonians, along with the Ephesians and Colossians, is the subject of dispute among critics, for the Pauline authorship of this letter is doubted.

> Since Baur's day the objections brought by the Tübingen school against the genuineness of the First Epistle to the Thessalonians, the Epistle to the Philippians and to Philemon have been shown to be untenable. These writings, in addition to the four main Epistles (Galatians, I, II Corinthians, Romans), may now be treated as unquestionably genuine.[3]

GALATIANS

Galatians deals with the major crisis in the history of the early church—the relation of Christianity to Judaism. This Judaizing party[4] contends that a Christian must submit to all the Jewish forms and ceremonies. Paul refuted this idea in the position that through Christ we gain the knowledge of God and not through the Laws and ceremonials of Judaism.

Paul wrote this epistle between A.D. 53 and 56, some time on his second missionary journey, after he had passed through Galatia and not later than during his visit to Corinth. Paul

---

[3] Albert Schweitzer, *The Mysticism of Paul the Apostle,* p. 41
[4] Acts 15.

rebukes the Galatians that they have turned so quickly from his teachings and his gospel of salvation by faith rather than by the works of the law. The need of the church in Galatia concerned the fundamental question which was to determine the life of Christianity as a distinct religion. The emotional strain under which this letter was written accounts for its rugged, incoherent style.

I AND II CORINTHIANS

I Corinthians was written to the church at Corinth to help the members make the adjustment of their Jewish heritage to Hellenistic culture and philosophy and to their loyalty to Christ. Paul wrote as many as four letters to the Corinthians:

1. The letter referred to in I Corinthians 5:9–13.
2. The letter known as I Corinthians.
3. The letter referred to in II Corinthians 2:4 f., which probably does not refer to either of the above.
4. The letter known as II Corinthians, or at least the first part of it.[5]

There were four divisions in the church at Corinth—the followers of Apollos, of Peter, of Paul, and of Christ. While on his third missionary journey at Ephesus in Asia Minor, Paul heard of the situation in the church at Corinth, which he had founded on his second missionary journey. Corinth, the city of pleasure, was the capital of Roman Greece, a wealthy commercial center. Party divisions, immorality, lawsuits, divorce, sacrifices, women, the Lord's Supper, spiritual gifts, the Resurrection and his personal greetings are the subjects which Paul discusses in I Corinthians.

The First Letter to the Corinthians had been sent by Titus, but when Titus returned to Ephesus and told Paul of the conditions in the Corinthian church, Paul wrote another vitriolic letter. To compensate for this letter, Paul again writes to defend his own ministry and to comfort those whom he had so severely rebuked, and this constitutes (at least a part of) our II Co-

---

[5] Wood and Grant, *The Bible as Literature,* p. 294.

rinthians. The first nine chapters overflow with kindness and goodness, but critics feel that the last four chapters constitute part of the "painful letter" of which Paul had spoken. These chapters are considered by scholars as an appendix to II Corinthians, for they are autobiographical. One of the best-known chapters in the Corinthian letters is the chapter on immortality from which we find, "O death, where is thy sting? O grave, where is thy victory?"[6]

The greatest piece of literature ever written is Paul's chapter on love. The closing verses are—

> For now we see through a glass, darkly; but then face
> to face; now I know in part; but then shall I know even
> as also I am known. And now abideth faith, hope,
> charity, these three; but the greatest of these is charity.[7]

ROMANS

Not long after the writing of the Corinthian letters, in A.D. 57, Paul, in the course of his third missionary journey, went to Corinth, where he remained for three months, and where he wrote his Epistle to the Romans. After his trouble with the Corinthian church, we see in Romans that Paul at long last is enjoying peace in the calm and quiet of a winter spent in Corinth.[8] In this peaceful atmosphere, Paul was able to give, in a logical, systematic way, a complete definition of his faith.

For a period of seven years, Paul had established churches in the eastern provinces. His plan now, was to devote himself to the West, and he felt that he must begin from Rome, the capital city of the world, where a church had been established, perhaps through the followers of Stephen. Knowing the background of the Jewish reactionaries in the churches in Corinth and Galatia, Paul felt that he must know whether or not the church at Rome would support him.

He had not been to Rome; he wrote to the members of a

---

[6] I Corinthians 15:55.
[7] I Corinthians 13:12–13.
[8] Acts 20:3.

church who were strangers to him. He was not dealing with definite problems in the Epistle to the Romans but was setting forth to this church the nature of his teaching and explaining his projected mission in the West. Hence, this epistle, in the form of a sermon, takes on the appearance of a theological treatise. Paul had a presentiment that his work was at an end and that if he were to set forth the summary of his teaching to the Roman church, these views would not only have a wide circulation but would also be preserved for future generations.

Romans treats in succession the Theology of Individual Salvation (Chapters 1–8) and the Theology of History (9–11).[9]

Paul had risked his life to secure unity between his churches and the Jerusalem church, and he was now eager to unify the whole series of Gentile churches from Antioch to Spain. The Epistle to the Romans is written to both the Hebrew Christians and to the Gentile Christians in Rome. In Rome, Christianity had begun as a Jewish movement, and the idea was embedded, even in the minds of the Gentile converts, that it was dependent on Judaism. Because Paul had broken with the Law, he was regarded with suspicion. Paul, in the Roman letter, quotes a number of Psalms and Isaiah 59 to show that through the Law came not justification but knowledge of sin. He further states that apart from the Law has come the righteousness of God through faith in Jesus. Paul maintains that faith, rather than the keeping of the Law, is the fundamental ground of hope.

He dwells on the privilege, vouchsafed to his readers, of inheriting the promises made to Abraham although they had no title to be considered his children. He even feels it necessary to plead for due acknowledgment of the claims of Israel on the part of those who were forgetful of their debt (11:13 f.). . . . The Gentiles had cultivated wisdom, with the result that the wisdom in which they trusted had ensnared them and led them

---

[9] H. K. Booth, *The Background of the Bible,* p. 168.

into ever deeper corruption (1:18–2:11). The Jews had placed their reliance on the Law, but the Law, while it pointed the way to life, had given men no power to follow it and had left them more miserable than before (2:12–3:20). There remains only the method of faith which Christ has revealed and which avails alike for Jew and Gentile (3:21–31). . . . Long before the Law was given, Abraham had put his faith in God, and on this ground God had accepted him.[10]

Critics question parts of chapters 15 and 16 and feel that parts of these chapters may be fragments of other Pauline letters which were attached to Romans in the manuscripts. The tone is different in these chapters, and the friends addressed could scarcely have been in Rome at this time.

On Paul's third missionary journey he visited all of the churches previously founded in Asia Minor and in Greece. The writer of Acts devotes much of his time to a description of Paul's three-year ministry in Ephesus. It was here that Paul wrote I and II Corinthians. When he left Ephesus he went to Troas and into Macedonia, where he began his last journey through Greece, taking up on this trip a collection[11] for the poverty-stricken church in Jerusalem. When he reached Corinth, he spent the winter there and wrote the Roman letter. At the close of the winter, Paul with a group of friends sailed from Corinth to Jerusalem, where he was attacked by a mob, and was taken secretly to Caesarea, where for two years he remained a prisoner. In A.D. 59 he was sent to Rome,[12] where he awaited trial for two years. The Book of Acts closes with this statement:

> And Paul dwelt two whole years in his own hired house, and received all that came unto him, preaching the kingdom of God, and teaching those things which concern the Lord Jesus Christ, with all confidence, no man forbidding him.[13]

---

[10] E. F. Scott, *The Literature of the New Testament,* pp. 162–65.
[11] Acts 20:1–4.
[12] Acts 27:1–28; 15.
[13] Acts 28:30–31.

PHILIPPIANS

The Romans treated their prisoners lightly and with much freedom. It was while Paul was imprisoned in Rome, about A.D. 62, that he wrote the four prison epistles ascribed to him, Philemon, Colossians, Ephesians and Philippians. Philippians was written to inform the church at Philippi how Paul fared as a prisoner.[14] Critics assume that there has been no editorial work or interpretations here. The style is the antithesis of Romans, for it is personal and informal; it follows no sequence of thought, and it deals with a special situation. Paul thanks the Philippian church for the gift of money which was made to him to help ameliorate his case. He sent his letter by Timothy, and the Philippian church chose Epaphroditus as its messenger to Paul.[15] Paul again reiterates his message of life, which includes works in itself, and of death, which means being with Christ.[16] Paul's fate is soon to be determined by Nero, and he hopes that he will soon be able to visit the church at Philippi; but the outcome of his trial is uncertain. He has given up the thought, so prominent in I Thessalonians, written ten years previously, of the visible return of Christ. He does not even mention in the Philippian letter his hope of being able to carry the Gospel to Spain. There are two alternatives left for him, either his release from prison or his death—which means, to him, to be with Christ. Whether Paul was set free we do not know. The record breaks off here, and we have only conjecture.

Philippi, in Macedonia, is the city in which Paul founded his first church in Europe. It is to this, his most beloved church, that he writes his last words. The Jewish enemies of Paul who had caused the discord in the Corinthian and Galatian churches had also been at work at Philippi. Paul writes to encourage and to counsel the Philippian church. One of the greatest expressions of the principle of the Christian life is embodied in the closing chapter of this letter:

. . . whatsoever things are true, whatsoever things are

---

[14] Philippians 1:12–26.
[15] Philippians 2:19–30.
[16] Philippians 1:12–26.

honest, whatsoever things are just, whatsoever things
are pure, whatsoever things are lovely, whatsoever
things are of good report; if there be any virtue, and if
there be any praise, think on these things.[17]

Our religion came through the channels prepared for it in
Judaism, and was molded by the philosophies prevalent in the
first century of the Roman Empire. Jewish and Hellenistic
thought, for all their apparent contrasts, were not so far apart.
Jewish and Greek thinkers worked on much the same problems.

By different paths they had arrived at ethical positions
which were broadly similar, so that it is often difficult to
say which of them may have suggested certain elements in New Testament teaching. They were at one
in their conviction that man on earth is shut out from
his true life and freedom, and that his great need is for
deliverance. As we read Plato we are constantly ar-
rested by ideas which seem to echo the Old Testament
and to anticipate the Gospels and Epistles. . . . There
is much in the Judaism of the first century which was
historically related to Hellenistic thinking. . . . Paul
himself mixes the two modes of thought, and never
doubts that in both of them he is seeking to express
the same truth. This confusion was possible only because, in the last resort, they were related. By their
different categories the Jew and the Hellenist were
intent on describing the same aspirations, the same conceptions of higher life. The Hellenistic attitude was
undoubtedly different from the Jewish, and our religion, by adopting it, changed its character.[18]

The debt, not only to literature but also to life, was im-
measurable when Paul's letters were published at Ephesus in
A.D. 90.

They gave to the early churches religious materials of
the utmost practical worth and greatly stimulated

---

[17] Philippians 4:8.
[18] E. F. Scott, *The Gospel and Its Tributaries*, pp. 273–74.

Christian literary expression. They preserved priceless memorials of the great pioneer missionary to the Greeks which were at the same time historical documents of the highest value for Christian origins. And without knowing it, they laid the foundation of the New Testament. . . . It is impossible to publish a collection of anyone's letters without editorial work of some kind. . . . That they found any considerable number of Paul's letters in existence and made a selection from them is unlikely; more probably they assembled and published all they could find. The only exception would be II Corinthians, which gave so painful a picture of both Paul and the Corinthians that we are not surprised to find it unknown to I Clement and so probably absent from the earliest form of the collection. It may have been the strong approval with which Clement in his letter to Corinth appeals to I Corinthians that led the Corinthians to bring out of their church chest the rest of their correspondence with Paul, combining his third and fourth letters to them into what we know as II Corinthians. . . . The Ephesian editors may have combined two letters to Philippi into our Philippians and added the short letter introducing Phoebe to the church at Ephesus to the great letter to the Romans— a thing all the more likely if Romans stood at the end of the collection.[19]

---

[19] Edgar J. Goodspeed, *The Formation of the New Testament*, pp. 30–32.

· IX ·

Conclusion

Toward the close of the second century the various primitive collections of letters and Christian books were gathered into a New Testament as a companion to the Old Testament. There were many ancient New Testaments, no one of which included all the doubtful books. There are various lists of books of the Bible given in the Clermont Manuscript, about A.D. 300, with dashes marking the doubtful books. A little later, Eusebius lists a number of books as rejected books. Fifty years later, the Sinaitic Manuscript of the Greek Bible issued a list. About A.D. 367 Athanasius includes in his list the Teaching of the Apostles and the Shepherd of Hermes as an appendix to the New Testament. The Alexandrian Manuscript, written in the fifth century, places I Clement and II Clement after the Revelation of John.

The letters of Paul had not been collected and published when Mark, Matthew, and Luke–Acts were written, though they were all written long before the first of our Gospels was produced.[1] Between the publication of Luke–Acts and that of Revelation, the Pauline letters were collected and published about A.D. 90. All subsequent Christian writings were either in

---

[1] Edgar J. Goodspeed, *New Chapters in New Testament Study.*

imitation of the Pauline corpus or reaction from it. The Revelation corpus is a general letter to the seven churches, followed by the Johannine corpus of one general letter, one to a church, and one to an individual. The Pauline corpus served as a model of the Ignatian corpus of seven letters, plus Polycarp as a covering letter.

Not until the fourfold Gospel Matthew, Mark, Luke, and John was published about A.D. 120–25 did the gospel type of writing develop rapidly and profusely. Gospels such as Hebrews, Egyptians, Peter, James, Thomas and others began to be written.

> The latter half of the New Testament and indeed the bulk of early Christian literature can be, to a large extent, genetically charted, as one book springs from and rests upon another. The early Christian world was, numerically speaking, a small world, kept in more or less close personal touch by its hopes and fears and its hospitalities. Its original literary poverty would lead to a rather general circulation of what few books it produced at first, so that we may expect these to operate upon those who followed them.[2]

When the ancient churches canonized from twenty-two to twenty-seven books of the New Testament, the other early Christian books were automatically condemned and disappeared; hence, much valuable literature perished. The canonization of the books of the New Testament tended to make of them a collection of books of equal authority. Modern critics now ask themselves who wrote each book, why and in what circumstances was it written, with what materials and for whom.

Thus we see that the New Testament is not only the literature of the early church but is also a selection from that literature. From this selection the disputed books were dropped, and the New Testament took its definite form when in A.D. 367 Athanasius, the foremost man in the whole church, enumerated

---

[2] *Op. cit.,* p. 70.

the twenty-seven books as we have them now in our New Testament. The New Testament, henceforth, dominated the Old Testament, which was interpreted to agree with the New.

> The Old Testament has exerted its living power and will exert it as long as men, thirsting for the revelation of the living God, read the pages of this book, which, together with the New Testament, has become the Bible of mankind, Israel's priceless literary bequest to the world.[3]

GENERAL SUMMARY

It has been the purpose of this study to make clear that the Bible is a product of many minds, of various ages, and of various viewpoints, that it is an anthology culled from a much larger literature, and that it is the record of the progressive revelation of God, with Christ as the final meaning.

We showed in this progressive revelation that from about 1050 to 850 B.C. the early histories and codes were composed, and that the prophetic narratives were begun. Following this period were the documents J in 850 B.C., E in 750 B.C., D in 650 B.C., and P from 586–37 B.C. (Babylonian Exile). With the Exile came the age of compilation. During this age the priesthood was dominant and interpreted the traditions of the past in the priestly interests. The age of editing and canonization followed the age of compilation, and we found that the Law became canonical in 444 B.C., that the Prophets became canonical about 200 B.C., and that the Writings became canonical in A.D. 90.

We showed that the Old Testament canon was the model on which the New Testament canon was formed. From about A.D. 30 to 40 oral traditions of Jesus' life were circulated in Aramaic, and much later traditions were circulated in Greek. Writers collected Jesus' sayings (called Logia), but these sayings were traditionally attributed to Matthew. Following this period, the Gospels in the order Mark, Matthew, Luke, and

---

[3] J. A. Bewer, *The Literature of the Old Testament*, p. 436.

John were written. The letters of Paul preceded the Gospels. At approximately the close of the Synoptic Gospel period were written the letters of James, Peter, and John, and the apocalyptic work Revelation—akin to the apocalyptic literature of Judaism, especially Daniel.

We showed that the canonization of the New Testament was like that of the Old Testament in that the disputed books were dropped before a final decision was made. In A.D. 367, the twenty-seven books as we have them now in our New Testament were enumerated by Athanasius, and the New Testament canon was closed.

The progressive revelation of God, climaxing in Christ and his teachings, has been the concept held throughout this study. This conception of the Bible appeals to the mind as well as to the heart.

Bibliography

Abingdon Bible Commentary, The, edited by Frederick Carl Eiselen, Edwin Lewis, and David G. Downey. Nashville: The Abingdon Press, 1929.

Bacon, S. W., F. C. Porter, and S. J. Case (editors). *Studies in Early Christianity.* New York and London: The Century Company, 1929.

Bewer, Julius A. *The Literature of the Old Testament in Its Historical Development.* New York: Columbia University Press, 1922.

Bible, The Holy (Authorized Version), edited by the Rev. C. I. Schofield. New York: Oxford University Press (American Division), 1917.

Bible Designed to Be Read as Living Literature, The, King James Version arranged and edited by Ernest Sutherland Bates. New York: Simon and Schuster, 1936.

Booth, Henry Kendall. *The Background of the Bible.* New York: Charles Scribner's Sons, 1928.

Bower, William Clayton. *The Living Bible.* New York: Harper and Brothers, 1936.

Bowie, Walter Russell. *The Story of the Bible.* Nashville: The Abingdon Press, 1934.

Brightman, Edgar Sheffield. *The Sources of the Hexateuch.* Nashville: The Abingdon Press, 1918.

Cadman, S. Parkes. *The Prophets of Israel.* New York: The Macmillan Company, 1933.

Catholic Encyclopedia, The (articles on Douay Bible, Bible, Abraham, Apocrypha, Septuagint, Versions of the Bible, etc.), special ed. The Encyclopedia Press.

Coffin, Henry Sloane. *The Portraits of Jesus Christ in the New Testament.* New York: The Macmillan Company, 1926.

Dibelius, Martin. *A Fresh Approach to the New Testament and*

Early Christian Literature. New York: Charles Scribner's Sons, 1936.

Easton, Burton Scott. *The Gospel Before the Gospels.* New York: Charles Scribner's Sons, 1928.

Encyclopædia Brittanica (articles on Septuagint, Laodicea, Jamnia, etc.), 14th ed. London: The Encyclopædia Britannica Company, 1929.

Excluded Books From the New Testament, The, translated by Lightfoot, James, Swete, with an introduction by J. Armitage Robinson. New York: Harper and Brothers.

Fowler, Henry Thatcher. *The History and Literature of the New Testament.* New York: The Macmillan Company, 1934.

Glover, T. R. *The World of the New Testament.* New York: The Macmillan Company, 1931.

Goodspeed, Edgar J. *The Formation of the New Testament.* Chicago: University of Chicago Press, 1926.

———. *The Making of the English New Testament.* Chicago: University of Chicago Press, 1925.

———. *New Chapters in New Testament Study.* New York: The Macmillan Company, 1937.

———. *New Solutions of New Testament Problems.* Chicago: University of Chicago Press, 1927.

———. *The Story of the Bible.* Chicago: University of Chicago Press, 1936.

———. *The Story of the New Testament.* Chicago: University of Chicago Press, 1916.

Gordon, T. Crowther, *The Rebel Prophet.* New York: Harper and Brothers, 1932.

Gore, Charles, H. L. Gaudge, and Alfred Guillaume (editors). *A New Commentary on Holy Scripture.* New York: The Macmillan Company, 1928.

Gregory, Casper Réné. *Canon and Text for the New Testament.* New York: Charles Scribner's Sons, 1929.

Gunkel, Hermann. *The Legends of Genesis,* translated by W. H. Carruth. Chicago: Open Court Publishing Company, 1901.

Hastings, James. *Dictionary of the Bible* (various articles). New York: Charles Scribner's Sons, 1909.

———. *Encyclopedia of Religion and Ethics* (articles on Antichrist, Gospels, Paul, Persecution, Gnosticism, etc.). New York: Charles Scribner's Sons, 1910.

Hodges, George. *How to Know the Bible*. Indianapolis: Bobbs-Merrill Company, 1918.

Hopwood, P. G. S. *The Religious Experience of the Primitive Church*. New York: Charles Scribner's Sons, 1937.

Jastrow, Morris Jr. *A Gentle Cynic*. Philadelphia and London: J. B. Lippincott Company, 1919.

———. *Job*. Philadelphia and London: J. B. Lippincott Company, 1920.

———. *Song of Solomon*. Philadelphia and London: J. B. Lippincott Company, 1921.

Jefferson, Charles E. *Cardinal Ideas of Jeremiah*. New York: The Macmillan Company, 1928.

Jewish Encyclopedia, The (articles on Jamnia, Talmud, etc.). New York and London: Funk and Wagnalls Company, 1916.

Knox, Raymond C. *Know the Bible*. New York: The Macmillan Company, 1936.

Knudson, Albert C. *The Beacon Lights of Prophecy*. Nashville: The Methodist Book Concern, 1914.

Lake, Kirsopp. *Paul, His Heritage and Legacy*. London: Christophers, 1934.

Lyman, Mary Ely. *The Christian Epic*. New York: Charles Scribner's Sons, 1936.

Moehlman, Conrad Henry. *The Christian-Jewish Tragedy*. Rochester, N. Y.: Printing House of Leo Hart, 1933.

Moffatt, James. *Introduction to the Literature of the New Testament*, 3d ed. New York: Harper and Brothers, 1918.

Moore, George Foot. *Judaism in the First Centuries of the Christian Era*, 2 vols. Cambridge: Harvard University Press, 1927.

Peake, Arthur S. *A Commentary on the Bible* (articles on Canon and Text of the Old Testament, Chronology of the New Testament, etc.). New York: Thomas Nelson and Sons, 1919.

Pearce, Abigail. *The Scriptures in the Making.* New York: The Macmillan Company, 1927.

Rice, John A. *The Old Testament in the Life of Today.* New York: The Macmillan Company, 1921.

Robinson, George L. *Where Did We Get Our Bible?* New York: Doubleday, Doran and Company, 1928.

Roth, Cecil. *A Bird's-Eye View of Jewish History.* Cincinnati: Union of American Hebrew Congregations, 1935.

Ryle, Herbert Edward. *The Canon of the Old Testament.* New York: The Macmillan Company, 1914.

Schweitzer, Albert. *The Mysticism of Paul the Apostle,* translated into English by William Montgomery. New York: Henry Holt and Company, 1931.

Scott, Ernest Findlay. *The Gospel and Its Tributaries.* New York: Charles Scribner's Sons, 1930.

———. *The Kingdom of God in the New Testament.* New York: The Macmillan Company, 1931.

———. *The Literature of the New Testament.* New York: Columbia University Press, 1932.

———. *The New Testament Idea of Revelation.* New York: Charles Scribner's Sons, 1935.

Smith, John Merlin Powis. *The Books of Amos, Hosea and Micah.* New York: The Macmillan Company, 1914.

Smyth, J. Patterson. *How We Got Our Bible.* New York: James Pott and Company, 1928.

Souter, Alexander. *The Text and Canon of the New Testament.* New York: Charles Scribner's Sons, 1912.

Streeter, Burnett Hillman. *The Four Gospels.* New York: The Macmillan Company, 1925.

Thowards, Thomas. *Comments on the Psalms.* New York: R. M. McBride and Company, 1929.

Trattner, Ernest R. *Unravelling the Book of Books*. New York: Charles Scribner's Sons, 1929.

Weymouth, R. F. *The New Testament in Modern Speech*. Boston: The Pilgrim Press, 1924.

Wicksteed, Joseph H. *A Study of Blake's Vision of the Book of Job*. New York: Dutton, 1924.

Willett, Herbert L. *The Bible Through the Centuries*. Chicago: Willett, Clark and Company, 1929.

————. *The Jew Through the Centuries*. Chicago: Willett, Clark and Company, 1932.

Wood, Irving Francis, and Elihu Grant. *The Bible as Literature*. Nashville: The Abingdon Press, 1914.

TWO